I0457890

Hello, Halo

Hello, Halo

Connect with the angels to strengthen your
faith, expand your beliefs, and get inspired!

HEATHER SPRIGG

Pen & Publish
Saint Louis, Missouri

Copyright © 2025 Heather Sprigg

All rights reserved. No part of this book may be reproduced or transmitted in any form or by any means, electronic or mechanical, including photocopying, recording, or by any information storage and retrieval system, without permission in writing from the publisher.

Published by Pen & Publish, LLC, USA

www.PenandPublish.com
info@PenandPublish.com

Saint Louis, Missouri
(314) 827-6567

Paperback ISBN: 978-1-956897-75-3
ebook ISBN:978-1-956897-76-0
Library of Congress Control Number: 2025947888

Cover design: Nathaniel Scripture, BlueTigerArts.com

*I am dedicating this book to the memory of my
late mentor, teacher, and friend, Pat Longo.*

*Pat was a beacon of light in my spiritual journey and I will
miss her more than words could ever convey. She was a huge
part of this book and I am so grateful that she got to read it
before she passed. Her approval meant the world to me.*

Dear Pat,

For the last eleven years you have been a constant source of support and strength for me. Throughout the years you went from mentor/teacher to friend and lastly to family. Although you weren't old enough to be my gramma, that is the energy we had together, so that is the role you stepped into. You opened your home, your heart, and even your recipe book to me. Thank you for the years of memories and for teaching me how to cook and bake like a Longo. I will be baking your signature chocolate and banana cream pies this Christmas in your honor. Speaking of Christmas, a holiday we both loved, I will never be able to watch a Hallmark movie without remembering how you would always fall asleep halfway through, then wake up about twenty minutes before the end. You always said you knew you didn't miss much since they all pretty much follow the same storyline ... then you would ask me to fill you in anyway.

You were always excited to be my guinea pig when I developed a new spiritual gift and always cheered me on when I accomplished something new. You were my cheerleader and because of you I am the person I am today. I will always remain humble and work with integrity just like you taught me, and I promise to continue to share with others all I have learned from you.

I miss and love you so much. Although I would rather have you here on Earth, I am honored to have you as one of the angels watching over me and my loved ones. Those in Heaven referred to you as the Dove, so until we meet again, I will look for doves to know you are near. Please send a few every now and then and say hi.

Love,

Heather

Contents

Introduction

L ike many kids, I grew up with a wild imagination. My parents always told me I could be whatever I wanted to be, and I believed them. I spent hours upon hours in my room imagining how my life was going to turn out. Depending on the day, I would dream of being a ballerina, hairdresser, model, teacher, or princess. I even had a whole magical crystal kingdom to rule over.

One thing I never dreamed of being, however, was an angel. Not only did it never cross my mind, I don't recall ever giving angels much thought at all. They simply weren't on my radar. When I look back now, I believe it was because as a child, a part of me remembered that I was an angel, so there was no need to dream or imagine being one.

Yes, you read that right: I am an incarnated angel. It wasn't until recently, however, that I learned to accept who I was and why I came here. You see, I didn't think angels incarnated on Earth. I had believed everything I read about them, including that they had no free will, had no personalities, had specific jobs to do that fit into nice little categories, and that they never walked the earth as humans. All of those assumptions were wrong. Through my years of channeling angels as an angel medium, I have discovered why I am here now, at this time. I am here to be a voice for the angels, restore faith, and help mankind build a relationship with the angels.

Before I go any further, there are some things I want to get out of the way. All the information I receive about angels comes from the angels themselves. I did not rely on what has already been written about them for this book. In fact, as I was writing this book, I was instructed not to read any books on angels. The angels didn't want me to be swayed or to seek validation from others. They wanted me to go straight to them, and since a lot of what I'm going to be covering in this book is new, they told me I wouldn't be able to find relevant sources anyway. Instead, the information in this book is meant to be validation for others who have always felt there was more to angels than what has been written. To say that this took a lot of trust is an understatement!

The topics in this book were chosen by the angels because they feel they are important for mankind to understand moving forward. We are in a time of huge transition and are currently laying the foundation for a new type of Earth and a new way of being. This next phase involves unlearning old belief patterns and focusing more on what brings us together instead of the fear that divides us. We were never meant to live in fear; we were meant to live in faith. God doesn't want His children brought to Him out of fear. He wants them brought to Him out of faith, love, and hope.

Although I work with all the angels, the angel I work most closely with, and who has been my partner in writing this book, is Archangel Michael. Throughout this book I refer to him simply as Michael. I also use the name God in this book. This is how I grew up referring to Him and not about a specific religion or gender. In the chapter about religion,

I go over why God and His angels were never meant to be placed into a religious category. God and His angels are not exclusive; they are inclusive.

As you'll soon notice, I've included my story of spiritual awakening as well as the challenges I faced along the way. The angels felt it was important for you to get to know me as well. So please sit back, relax, keep an open mind, and let the angels and me take you on a journey of the way our creator intended things to be. A journey out of the age of fear and into the age of clear.

Angel Message

"There is no time limit on childhood dreams."

The angels want to remind you that you are never too old to pursue your dreams, so keep dreaming.

—Heather Sprigg

1

In the Beginning

"Children see magic because they look for it."
—Christopher Moore

It may come as no surprise, but I didn't grow up knowing I could talk to angels, or that I was one. In fact, my first encounter with a spirit was rather traumatizing, enough so that I remember all the details to this day. I'm also pretty sure my parents remember it in detail too, although I'm sure they have tried to forget. (Sorry, Mom and Dad.) The first time I remember seeing a spirit, I was three years old. My baby sister, Gina, newly home from the hospital, was sleeping soundly in her crib in the room we shared. One night I heard voices, so I sat up and looked to my right. I saw two shadows shaped like two plump, older women. I still remember what they looked and sounded like to this day.

"Oh, look at the baby," one of them said. I jumped out of my bed and ran screaming at the top of my lungs across the hall and into my parents' room. I screamed that someone was in our room with the baby. They, of course, were very alarmed and ran across the hall to find the room empty with Gina, surprisingly, still sound asleep.

After that, I don't remember seeing spirits as a child again. I do, however, remember my magical kingdom in the clouds. Whenever I had time, I'd escape to my crystal castle in the sky. I named it Crystalia and called the people Crystallines. Now, keep in mind I didn't know anything about crystals or crystalline light bodies. My parents weren't into crystals or spiritual theories and thought I just made the word up. I just knew this magical kingdom in the sky was a place where I felt comfortable, like I was at home. I would sit on my bedroom floor with my legs crossed and rock back and forth. My parents actually thought there was something wrong with me since I'd spend hours rocking. I believe it was my younger self's way of getting into a meditative state. But hey, whatever it was, it worked for me! It wasn't until years later that I realized I wasn't imagining my magical kingdom at all. I had actually been there many times. I believe I was remembering my time in the seventh dimension (more on this later) with the angels. I go there often when I meditate now (minus the rocking), and guess what I see when I do? I see crystals!

Besides magical kingdoms, my childhood was pretty ordinary. I was born in Olympia, Washington, and lived the first sixteen years of my life in a sleepy little town named Chehalis. Most of the people in Chehalis and the surrounding areas were farmers. When I was sixteen, my family moved to an even smaller farming town in the middle of nowhere, called Winlock, Washington. This is where they live to this day, and where I consider home. My dad was a police officer, firearms instructor, and sniper on the SWAT team, and my mom was a stay-at-home mom for the first part of my childhood, until she became a commissioned police sergeant at the local jail. As you can see, helping others runs in the family. I actually have a criminology degree to fall back on if this angel thing doesn't work out! I decided a while ago that instead of a gun and Kevlar vest, I would carry sage and crystals. Gina is also spiritually connected, and as a child she, too, would see spirits, but so far it has not become part of her path.

Going to School

I was a homebody even as a young child. I didn't attend play-dates or even preschool, so kindergarten was my first experience away from home and my parents. Boy, was that a shock to my little system! It was overwhelming to be around so many other kids. To say I was a shy child would be an understatement. I was so shy I was afraid to talk in class. Being called on was my biggest fear and not because I didn't know the answers (I usually did) but because people would look at me, which made me so uncomfortable. By the time I was in third grade, I was diagnosed with dyslexia and placed in a class with others like me. I was also put into speech therapy since I had trouble pronouncing words. I could hear them in my mind, and say them in my mind, but there was a disconnect between my mind and my mouth. The words just never came out sounding right. This made me even more self-conscious as a child. Eventually, I learned a new way to read, write, and do math so that no one could tell I was dyslexic, and by the fourth grade I was placed back into regular classes. The year of separation, however, left me feeling like I didn't fit in and that something was wrong with me. I always felt no one liked me. I did have friends, and no one was telling me they didn't like me, but I just didn't feel comfortable. It reached the point where I was picking up on everyone's vibes, which often conflicted with my own. This caused me to feel like every angry person was angry at me, every sad person was sad because of me, etc. It made being at school simply overwhelming. I often stayed home due to having an upset stomach. I couldn't really explain it; I just didn't feel right. Does any of this sound familiar? It turns out I am a sensitive empath, and unfortunately, no one really knew what that was back in the 1980s.

According to my mentor and spiritual teacher, Pat Longo, an empath is someone who is highly sensitive to the energies of others. They can feel the emotions, energy, mood, and pain as if it were their own (*The Gifts Beneath Your Anxiety*, Pat Longo). Since I didn't know I was an empath, I also didn't know how to differentiate between the energy and emotions of others versus my own. As you can imagine, that created a lot of challenges in the most important stages of my early life.

By the time I was in high school, I had learned to cope with, even suffocate, what I thought were my own feelings. After all, I assumed everyone felt the same way I did. When I became too overwhelmed, I would sit on the floor, rocking back and forth, and visit my magical kingdom. An interesting fact: Divine energy enters our crown chakra (top of our head) in a circular motion, like a funnel. That's why many channels and mediums sometimes rock back and forth, side to side, or in a circular motion when working with energy. So my rocking meant I was really getting into the flow!

During my freshman year I tried out for the cheerleading squad. To my surprise I made it, but I wasn't particularly skilled at it. I could do the cheers and dance routines on my own, when no one was watching, but once I got in front of an audience, all the energy of those around me would hit me and I'd become overwhelmed and get sick to my stomach. You see, not only was I feeling my own nervous energy, I was feeling the whole darn squad's nervous energy. As you can imagine, that combination didn't make for a good cheerleader. Nonetheless, I remained a cheerleader until my senior year, but I did what so many empathic children do: self-medicate. You see, the empathic child is feeling all these feelings that no one understands and so they try to control it themselves to numb the spiritual gifts they don't understand and to try to feel "normal." A lot of children turn to alcohol, drugs, self-harm, or even overexercising (to name a few). For me, it was an eating disorder. I may not have been able to control what I was feeling, but I could control what I was eating. I could eat anything I wanted to suffocate the feelings and then throw it up later so I wouldn't get fat. This feeling of control continued for fifteen years and created a sense of relief for me. Once I graduated from high school, I enrolled in a local community college. It wasn't long before the feeling of overwhelm from high school came back full force. I also became sick frequently and ended up dropping out after two terms. Remember the energy absorbed from being an empath? Well, according to Pat, the energy has to go somewhere once it enters your physical body. Many times, this energy comes out as an illness. Apparently, mine was coming out as kidney stones, one right after the other. Once I dropped out, the kidney stone pain subsided. I remember thinking, "What a coincidence."

All Grown Up

When I was twenty years old, I moved to Colorado. This is where I met a handsome blue-eyed boy named Davie. Davie was my knight in shining armor. He never judged me and loved me just the way I was. When I was twenty-one years old, I became pregnant with our first son, Cameron. It is important for me to mention that the only time I was able to quit my eating disorder was when I was pregnant with my boys. Caring for them gave me a sense of purpose and direction. For those amazing months, my eating disorder completely vanished—I felt free to be me. My only focus was on my baby. It was like the universe was giving me a break so that I could be a mom. After a few years in Colorado, Davie and I moved to Beaverton, Oregon, and welcomed our second baby boy, Dylan. Now our family was complete. I happily threw myself into being a stay-at-home mom and wife.

Once the boys were both in school full time, I even enrolled back in college. This time as a fully online student (baby steps) at a local university. Things were beginning to look up! Until they weren't. In November 2014, nothing out of the ordinary was going on in my life; I was just busy with school and being a mom. Then, all of a sudden, I developed an extreme case of anxiety. I'm talking about the kind that paralyzes you to the core, and provides you with enough mom guilt to last a lifetime. I was inexplicably anxious and scared, and I had no idea what triggered this deep fear. It appeared during the holiday season, which is usually my favorite time of year. While I was in the middle of planning all of our holiday crafts, baking, and adventures, I became too anxious to do anything. All my planning came to a sudden stop. Instead of making pumpkin bread and Christmas cookies with the boys, I would just sit on the couch for hours, afraid to do anything. Thankfully, the boys were too busy with school activities and friends to really notice Mom was acting strange. At this point I'd been back at college for a couple of years, working on my criminology and criminal justice degree. I had lost interest in my school work and, for the first time, thought about quitting. My anxiety was really messing with my mind. Then things got even worse when I became too anxious to leave the house. We live a mile from the kids' school, but I couldn't make myself leave the house to go pick them up. Instead, my husband had to leave his job, drive twenty minutes to pick them up and bring them home, then drive twenty minutes back to work. Davie never complained and just did what he had to do to help me. He was so worried and felt so helpless. Either the guy is a saint, or he did something really bad and I was his punishment. Looking back, I realize that I should have reached out to my friends and neighbors for help. But I was ashamed, and I had become paranoid that they didn't like me anymore. I had hit rock bottom and was more alone than ever, even while surrounded by loved ones. I would sometimes sit on the couch and open and close my hands over and over while softly whimpering to myself. It was my strange way of trying to cope and comfort myself when my anxiety was at its worst. I later learned those episodes were most likely panic attacks.

Along Came Pat Longo

Eventually, I decided to go to the doctor for help. Up until this point, I had hoped that my episodes would just end, but they continued to get worse. The doctor prescribed a powerful medication called Klonopin. Klonopin has many uses and side effects, but for me, it was to treat my anxiety. My prescription was for one to two pills a day, as needed. They helped for a while, but a couple months later, I was taking three to four a day just so I could function as a wife and mom. I began desperately praying for help. Every time I would pray for help, I would hear, "Call Pat Longo." I remembered thinking, "Great, now I'm hearing voices as well as going crazy." I had heard the name Pat Longo mentioned previously in Theresa Caputo's books (the Long Island Medium). Pat was Theresa's spiritual adviser and mentor. This intrigued me, so I started researching her. It turns out, Pat was a spiritual healer and teacher. I noticed on her website that she offered phone appointments, but I just couldn't wrap my head around her being able to help me over the phone. My anxiety, as well as my financial situation, was also stopping me from flying to Long Island, New York, for an in-person session. I tried to forget about it, but her name kept popping into my head every time I prayed for help. So, I took a leap of faith and decided to email her office to ask about getting an appointment over the phone. My expectations were pretty low to be honest, but little did I know, this appointment was about to change my entire life. I'd been told some people have had to wait months to reserve time with Pat. However, the angels had other plans. I messaged her office on a Friday, and as fate would have it, she had a cancellation for the following Monday. She had just received a call from a client who postponed their visit. Talk about a sign from above! My appointment was on April 18, 2015. This was the day that officially changed my life forever.

When it came time for my call, I was so excited, yet nervous and a bit skeptical. As soon as I heard her voice, however, all my doubts vanished. I was immediately put at ease. Pat listened to my story and asked me questions about my life. I couldn't stop talking . . . everything, all of it, just came flooding out. Someone was listening to me. Finally, someone understood. By the end of the hour-long appointment, I had my "diagnosis": not only was I going through what is referred to as a spiritual awakening, I was diagnosed as an empath and apparently a psychic medium. I found out that my anxiety was due to spirits trying to communicate with me, but being blocked instead of getting through. I also learned that the cough I'd had since childhood is what Pat called a "spirit cough." The energy from the spirits was getting caught up in my throat and causing the cough. (Not because I was swallowing spirits. And yes, I did ask.) My parents spent a lot of money on copays throughout the years trying to figure out that cough. Pat also taught me how to ground my energy and protect myself from the energies of others. This is a very important step for empaths or highly sensitive people (see Energetic Exercises at the end of Chapter 11).

During the last part of our appointment, Pat performed a remote healing on me. She cleared and aligned my physical, emotional, mental, and spiritual bodies and removed years of stagnant energy that had built up in my body over time. Before this appointment I had suffered from what I (and my doctors) thought was fibromyalgia. After this appointment, my fibromyalgia symptoms vanished into thin air. Pat said my illness was caused by a buildup of toxic energy in my body, which was now gone. When too much energy builds up in our bodies, it has nowhere to go. Since energy cannot be destroyed, only transformed, it often manifests as physical ailments. That's where we get the word *disease*: "dis-ease" in the body. Another benefit to my session with Pat was that my anxiety was instantly gone! That very day I was able to go out to lunch with my family like a normal person! I will never forget it. Dylan's birthday had been the day before, and he wanted all of us to go get waffles in downtown Portland with him. I was able to go downtown and celebrate with my family. I not only felt like a new person, but I felt like that was the day my boys got their mom back.

Hello, Spirits!

After my session with Pat, the spirits didn't waste any time. The very next morning, while Davie and the boys were getting ready (I was in that not-quite-asleep-but-not-quite-awake state), all of a sudden I heard this loud buzzing in my head and then my body began to physically shake. Even though I knew what was happening, it still freaked me out. I asked them to please stop, and they did, for a second anyway. This happened two more times before I started begging my spirit guides to please make them leave me alone. Not one of my braver moments, but I was legitimately scared. I also felt like I was a miserable failure. I contacted Pat later that morning and she told me I hadn't failed, that I could ask my spirit guides to introduce things to me at a slower pace—one that I was comfortable with. She also agreed that making me shake was unnecessary, but they really wanted to communicate. Can you imagine how my kids or husband would have felt if they had walked in while I was shaking? Luckily there hasn't been a single shake since . . . I think they got the message.

Over the next few months I began learning better ways of interacting with the spirits. Communicating is like a game of charades sometimes. They often use a combination of words, phrases, images, and feelings to get their message across. Since I'm an empath, they also make me feel things, such as how they had died. For example, one spirit made my chest tighten almost to the point I couldn't breathe. They were letting me know they passed from a heart attack. Another one made me feel like I was hit in the head. My husband didn't find any of this funny, by the way. He had to pay for all of my "mysterious" medical bills. This also explains a lot of my random trips to the doctor when I was younger. I was always thinking I was dying, but they could never figure out what was wrong with me.

Not long after getting used to the idea of having spirits around all of the time, I was given an opportunity to deliver my first message to someone outside of my family. During a hair appointment, as I was sitting under the dryer minding my own business, I began coughing nonstop. (That darn spirit cough was back again.) I also felt the anxiety return, and to make matters worse, I felt like I was going to either throw up or have diarrhea. (The glamorous world of mediumship!)

I had a feeling it was a spirit trying to come through, so I grounded my energy, took a deep breath, built up the courage, and said to myself, "Let's do this!" At this point I was now getting my hair rinsed when I suddenly envisioned an older lady happily waving to me. She wasn't full size; she was like Barbie doll size, and I was seeing her in my mind's eye. She wore black leggings, black flats, a loose black cotton long-sleeved top, hoop earrings, curly gray hair, and pink lipstick. To this day I still remember all the details. Now for the awkward part: I had no idea if my hairdresser believed in any of this. So I nonchalantly said, "Do you believe in mediums?" I was so relieved when she said yes, but I still needed to relay the message. I then described what I was seeing and feeling. Besides feeling this older woman's energy, I was also picking up on her personality. I don't know how I know that I'm even feeling "personality," but it just happens. I told her this woman was fun and bubbly and the life of the party. Thankfully, my hairdresser recognized the spirit as her grandmother who had recently passed. I didn't get much of a message—I was still fairly new—but just knowing she was there, at peace and happy, was a huge relief to her granddaughter. It was also a huge relief for me, especially since I didn't have an uncontrolled attack of diarrhea. I still had a lot to learn, but I had taken the first step and trusted what I was getting! I had communicated with a spirit, relayed a message, and brought my hairdresser some much-needed peace.

Angel Message

"Why compare yourself to others when your own light shines just as beautiful as the next?"

Each time we compare ourselves to someone else, whether it be a job, income, talents, appearance, or spiritual abilities, we create an energetic barrier that keeps our light from fully shining through and robs the world of our beautiful light and unique gifts.

—Heather Sprigg

2
I'm a What??

*"To be nobody—but yourself—in a world which is
doing its best, night and day, to make you everybody
else—means to fight the hardest battle which any
human being can fight; and never stop fighting."*

—E. E. Cummings

As I walked down the hallway of Dylan's high school, I spotted Stephanie ahead of me, standing alone in the common area. When she turned toward my direction, her face lit up in a way I've never seen before. Her eyes were wide and filled with awe; it was almost like she was in a peaceful trance. I remember thinking, "Wow, my ten-pound weight loss must really be noticeable!" I know, I know, wishful thinking, but a girl can hope. As I approached her, her face remained the same. No recognition—it was the strangest thing. "Stephanie, are you OK? It's Heather, Dylan's mom."

And just like that, she snapped back to reality. She shook her head and looked at me with some semblance of disappointment. "Oh ... Heather, it's you." Not knowing what else to say, I asked her who she thought I was. She said, "Please don't laugh, but I didn't see *you*. I saw an angel in all white light walking toward me." She was slightly embarrassed and disappointed. I'd be disappointed too if I thought an angel was walking toward me, only to realize it was just a mere human. What neither of us realized at the time was that there really was an angel walking toward her that day. That was the first time someone had seen me as I am, an angel, and it wouldn't be the last.

At this point in my spiritual journey, I was starting to join psychic development groups and take classes to further my spiritual education. I had just graduated from college at the ripe age of forty-three and had decided not to continue on to law school. This was actually a hard decision for me. I had always felt my calling, my purpose, was to be a voice for those who no longer had one. Since I come from a law enforcement family, I wanted to continue the family tradition, but to do it in my own way. I felt being a prosecutor was the perfect fit for me. (According to Davie I'd have made a great lawyer, since I like to argue and always think I'm right.) As I'm sure many of you can relate, suddenly finding yourself heading in a new, unknown direction can be scary. I felt a bit lost, like my whole identity was melting away. I even grieved for the life I always thought I'd have. Luckily, I had Pat Longo, my mentor, to help me along the way. I remember telling her how I wanted to use my spiritual gifts while being a lawyer. She laughed at me and said, "We'll see." She then told me that not everyone had to use their gifts as a career, but some of us were meant to. She felt strongly that I was in the latter category. She also told me she saw me writing a book. Looks like she was right on both counts. Not long after our conversation, I was in a deep meditative trance when these "light beings" appeared. (I didn't know they were angels at the time since they didn't appear with wings.) Without knowing what I was doing, my arms went out in front of me and started doing exactly what they were showing me how to do. They were showing me how to use different colors of energy to heal different ailments within myself and others. Although I was speechless and in a state of shock afterward, at the time it just felt normal for me to be in my living room learning from divine beings. It wasn't until much later that I realized I was learning from the angels and what they were teaching me. I learned that I could use colors to heal myself and others. They taught me that the color I used wasn't as important as the intention I set. For example, I find light blue calming, so when I wanted to calm someone's anxiety, I'd call upon Archangel Haniel and ask to use her calming blue energy. I would then form her energy into a ball between my hands and place it into the client. Talk about hands-on learning! I've included an energy ball exercise at the end of this chapter for you to try. I know this may sound confusing, but I believe it will make more sense after you give it a try for yourself.

This experience triggered the healing phase of my spiritual journey. I wanted to learn all I could about healing. This is what led me to enroll in a crystal reiki master class course. This is where I learned all about the healing powers of crystals, and although I don't use reiki when I do healings, I still use crystals when needed. Pat told me she felt the reason I was drawn to this course was to get reacquainted with crystals. And wouldn't you know it, she was right; as soon as she said that I remembered my magical crystal kingdom.

After I was satisfied with what I knew about healing from the angels, crystals, and Pat, I was ready to learn more. So I signed up for a twelve-week channeling course.

Now, I didn't even know what channeling was, but I knew I felt like I needed to take this course. In the months leading up to the course, I joined a Facebook group run by the instructors. There I would join Facebook Lives (online streaming events where practicing psychics, intuitives, mediums, and healers could go "live" in the Facebook group and practice reading others who were watching). I even had others give me readings, which helped me see the different ways people work. One reader after another started telling me they saw me with angel wings. As I listened to them read others, I realized this wasn't common; it wasn't happening to other students. In fact, I didn't hear them mention it to anyone else.

My curiosity was beginning to grow. Could I really be an angel? Do they even incarnate on Earth? After all, I had read books by well-known spiritual teachers who claimed they didn't. Sometimes the only way to receive accurate information is to go within and tap into divine knowledge. So back to meditation I went. Once again I went straight into a trance state (a state of deep meditation where the person is semi-conscious—almost like sleepwalking). Not long after reaching this state, I sat up, walked to the kitchen, grabbed a stack of computer paper and a pencil, and started drawing. I could tell I was drawing, but had no control over my hands and couldn't see what I was drawing since my eyes were closed. When I eventually snapped out of the trance, I looked down and saw roughly fifteen pages full of angel wings. Front and back. I was starting to actually allow myself to believe, to allow the possibilities to take shape. After that odd experience, I asked the angels to give me other signs that I couldn't ignore (you know, like hit me over the head with them). In the coming days, more intuitives and mediums told me I had wings, and suddenly I started hearing song lyrics in my head, like "Ohhh, you're an angel" over and over. Every time I would open my phone there would be something about angels on there. Once, it opened to a map with the business

"Visiting Angels" highlighted. Despite all these validations, I still needed more.

By this time, the channeling course had started. I learned that channeling is a form of mediumship, but unlike traditional mediumship where you have the spirit relay information to you, then you relay it to the client (kinda like a monkey in the middle), the spirit speaks through you. You become the channel, the conduit, a divine messenger of sorts. Automatic writing is also a form of channeling. This is where the angel, or other being, takes over your thoughts while writing. Instead of using your voice, they use your hand. During class a fellow student asked me if she could do a channeled reading on me. She channeled angels and felt called to read me. During this reading I asked her what my soul's origin was. They kept taking her back further and further in time. Back to the beginning. They then showed her me as an angel. To say she was shocked would be an understatement. That was the first time she realized angels can incarnate on Earth. I finally had all the proof I needed. Now it was time to tell Pat and see what she thought. As you can tell, Pat has played a huge role in my life. She once again surprised me by not being surprised. You see, Pat also did past-life regressions, and it often came up.

After many years, in 2023, I was finally able to meet her in person. While I was there she did a past-life regression on me. My higher self came through. When she asked who she was talking to, my higher self told her a seraphim angel. By this time I had already embraced being an angel for a few years, but I now had validation as to what kind I was. Seraphim angels typically stay close to God and are often involved in the creation process. According to the angels, they don't incarnate as often as other angels and because of this, when they do, they often appear to be young souls. They tend to act a lot younger than they are and find joy in all the little things that make up Earth. They aren't cynical yet. The example the angels gave me was of a new police officer. All eager to start and believing the best in everyone. Believing that they can save and fix everyone and change the world. The angels who incarnate more tend to be like the seasoned cop. They understand humans a bit more, and although they still want to make a difference, they realize some things can't be fixed by others.

Knowing I am an angel and accepting it are two separate things. Everything I had read about angels made me not want to be one. I had read they had no free will, and they had no personalities. I had also read that they didn't have soul families (groups of souls who often incarnate together and hang out in Heaven). The thought of going back to Heaven and not being able to be with my Earth family, my boys, was depressing. I actually cried and tried to get the angels to tell me they were wrong, that I was not an angel. During my channeling course I realized I was really good at channeling angels. It was like second nature to me. So I began talking with them and asking lots of questions. I wanted to know everything they knew, and I wanted to learn about all of them. I was relieved to find out they have free will too . . . and even personalities!! Each angel I channeled had their own unique energy and personality. For example, Archangel Azrael is like a stern father, while Archangel Haniel was softer and more nurturing. I also learned that angels do have soul families, and that although I'll go back to a different dimension (explained in a later chapter), I will still be close with my family in Heaven. I even found an angel brother in the channeling class. I had asked the angels to please connect me to another incarnated angel so I wouldn't feel so alone. They did; it turns out they had led another incarnated angel to that channeling course as well. His name is Nathaniel (Nate) Scripture (how fitting), and he has become a confidant and one of my best friends. He feels like a brother to me, and reminds me of home in the angelic dimensions. Nate is one of the more seasoned angels, like the experienced cops. He's likely spent many lives incarnating on Earth doing his own spiritual missions. He helps keep me grounded and reminds me of the challenges we face here as incarnated angels. After finding this out, I was ready to fully embrace being an angel.

This information, of course, led to its own set of challenges. If I was going to be a voice for the angels, I was going to have to come out as one. This caused me a lot of fear actually. The shy kid is still in there, after all. Luckily, my family was pretty understanding. Davie has always had an open mind and had already seen what I could do as a medium. So the jump to actual angel and angel medium wasn't a hard one for him to make. I believe his soul started to remember that he'd signed up for this crazy life with me. Either that, or it was just easier to go along with his crazy wife, but he was happy that I was happy. My kids, on the other hand, were a different story. They were already older: Cameron was in college getting a degree in chemistry and Dylan was in high school. I remember the first time I did a healing on someone from home. Davie described the looks on the boys' faces as a mixture of amusement and confusion as they watched their mom sit with her eyes closed and start moving her arms all around. It became even more apparent to them that their mom wasn't like their friends' moms when they would have to ask me what category to put me under when filling out forms for school. Dyl would ask, "Mom, what exactly do I say you do?" We went with small business owner since there wasn't a category for angel medium.

ANGEL LESSON   Energy Ball Exercise:

Start with rubbing your palms together to wake up the energy centers in your hands.

Now open and close your hands (like you are clapping), as if you are making one big ball of energy coming out from the center of your palms. (You actually are.)

After doing this a few times, slowly bring your hands together until you feel a slight resistance. This is your energy ball.

Go ahead and toss your energy ball to a loved one, or imagine pulling it back into your palms, and say, "Please, God, allow me to be a clear vessel of Your healing love, light, and energy. Please send a beam of Your white light through my crown chakra, through my body, and out my hands."

Now you are ready to make another energy ball. Notice the difference in how it feels? Notice the energy between your hands? Now start to close your hands and feel for the resistance. Notice how much bigger your energy ball is? That's because you are using God's energy and not just your own. Pretty cool, right?

Angel Message

"Release the need for validation from others. You don't need outside sources to validate your decisions, actions, dreams, or beliefs. You never did."

—Heather Sprigg

3

Angels

*'Do not forget to show hospitality to strangers,
for by so doing some people have shown
hospitality to angels without knowing it."*

—Hebrews 13:2

Once I fully accepted I was an angel, I realized I didn't know what it truly meant to be an angel. I know that the Bible says they are messengers of God and that they come to remind mankind of His love for us and that He is always near. I also know that they are protectors and bringers of light. All of this I have found to be true, but all it really answers is what they do; I still didn't know *who* they actually were. So I did exactly what they told me to do: When I needed an answer, I asked them.

"Angels are divine beings of light that are closest to God's energy. They work directly under God and are a part of God, as are you all. Angels are often thought of as messengers of God, but they are so much more. They play an active role

in the development of souls. They assist in whatever way is needed, for mankind and other beings as well. Think of them as loved ones who always have your back and are available to assist in whatever manner is needed. Their love for you is infinite. They take joy in watching you grow and learn and are your biggest cheerleaders. Angels were created from God to aid in the growth and development of His beings."

—The Angelic Collective
Channeled by Heather Sprigg, December 21, 2021

This was a great start, but I still wanted to know more. At this point in my journey, I was beginning to remember who I was. It was a familiarity about angels that I can't really explain, but it was felt deep within, by the part of me that knows who I am and why I'm here. It was starting to whisper the answers to all my questions through my soul. In these whispers, the truth about angels was slowly starting to be unveiled. I was starting to recognize the misinformation about them when I'd hear it or read it. Although I can't fit everything I have learned into this book, nor is this book the place to introduce it all, I have worked with the angels to figure out what they want you to know about them at this time. To help you get to know the real angels and why they are here to assist and support mankind—both incarnated angels and the angels still in Heaven.

Before I go any further, I'd like to go over the difference between what are referred to as Earth angels and incarnated angels. An Earth angel isn't an angel as traditionally known, but they still deliver messages from God and His angels still in Heaven. They are someone who does good in the world and assists in making it a better place. They are the souls on Earth that play such a big role in spreading love and faith and are considered most precious by the angels. You don't have to be an incarnated angel to be an Earth angel; in fact, most aren't. Earth angels are usually, but not always, sensitive to the spirit world so it is easier for God, His angels, and souls in Heaven to whisper in their ear. An incarnated angel is an actual Heavenly angel who chooses to come to Earth in human form to assist mankind. How they go about this often depends on the kind of angel they are, meaning what God created them for and their roles in Heaven. This can range from assisting individuals with their goals for personal soul growth to assisting mankind to evolve as a whole so they can rise in a collective frequency. Each role is just as important as the next, just like each soul on Earth has just as important a role to fulfill.

Angelic Roles

Although there is a lot written about specific angelic roles for each angel, the angels want to get away from that. For this reason I won't be going into each angel's "assigned" role. The angels say that when mankind has trouble understanding something new, they like to come up with categories and specific examples to make it easier to grasp. For example, many people believe that Archangel Michael offers only protection, while Archangel Raphael offers only healing. Until recently this misconception was fine with the angels, since they didn't work one-on-one with humans as often as they do now, and will continue to do in the future. They stayed in the background and worked mostly unnoticed behind the scenes.

Let's go back to the time of Atlantis (an ancient civilization of advanced beings on Earth), when the angels and the Atlanteans worked closely together. The angels could be physically seen, since the Atlanteans had collectively raised their frequency to such a high level, along with that of Earth. I'm not an expert on Atlantis, so I'm only going to go over what is necessary for this book. Eventually Atlantis fell, or became no more, and mankind had to start over (again, a very simplified explanation). The angels say we are now in the foundational stages of a large jump in frequency. This large jump in frequency is why so many are now realizing they are able to communicate with souls in Heaven and the angels. It is now time for the angels to have a more personal relationship with all of us. Because of this, many souls are choosing to work with a specific angel, or a group of them, as part of their soul contract. So instead of going to a different angel for each of your distinct needs, you have one angel (or a team of angels) who want to work with and assist you. If this is confusing, and you are wondering why they went along with the categories in the first place, then you are not alone. Since I like to have them explain things in simple terms, this is how they explained it: Think of the different time periods of mankind's evolution as grade levels. A kindergartener may learn simple addition, such as $1 + 1 = 2$. Then when they enter first grade, they expand upon that and start to add more numbers. This doesn't mean that what they learned in kindergarten is no longer relevant. It just means that now that the foundation was laid (or now that they have the necessary understanding), they are ready to advance to first grade. Then eventually they move on to multiplication, which again is only possible because of the foundations laid previously. Similarly, the knowledge learned previously through soul growth has led mankind to be ready to advance. The old information is still relevant, but we are at a new level of understanding. With each new layer, one is able to reach a higher frequency which allows for a stronger connection to those in Heaven and the angelic realms.

As we begin this monumental journey, the role of angels in our lives is evolving. The angels want to have personal working relationships with us. Because of this, the individual categories man has placed the angels in need to be dissolved. For example, before I incarnated, Archangel Michael and I agreed to work closely together. Because of this, he is the one I tend to go to for most things. If I need protection, someone to talk to, healing, comfort, etc., I call upon Archangel Michael. Each archangel can do what the others can. I mean, would you really think Archangel Gabriel or Ariel couldn't protect you? When you look at it that way, you can start to see why these categories don't really make sense. Don't get me wrong, though; they did have a purpose and worked really well for our ancestors. They didn't have the same relationships with the angels as we are meant to have now, so having specific jobs for each angel worked for them.

All this being said, angels still have their own personalities and energy. So there are certain angels I gravitate to when a client will ask me who to call to, let's say, comfort a broken heart. If I don't know who they are meant to work with, I'll suggest Archangel Haniel because her energy feels loving and nurturing and she enjoys working with issues of the heart. This doesn't mean another angel can't offer comfort, but that is the role she fills for me. (She is also one of the angels I am contracted to work with.) I also find that a lot of clients who are being called to work with nature and animals tend to be Archangel Ariel people. She enjoys helping with nature and animals and contracts to work with souls who are incarnating to work in those areas. Bottom line: Work with whom you feel most comfortable. If you don't yet know which angel you are supposed to work with, ask them to make themselves known to you and they will. This can be through an inner knowing, seeing their name or image pop up all over the place, or even dreaming of them.

Different Kinds of Angels

Although all angels were created to assist God and His souls, there are different types of angels. I'm told there isn't a hierarchy like many believe (remember mankind's love for neat categories?), but it's more about what they were created by God to do. Each kind of angel has just as important a role as the others. I'm told God doesn't have favorites; He loves all His creations the same.

I'm told that the first angels God created are what we call seraphim angels. Seraphims remain closest to God and assist Him in the creation and repairing of souls when needed (such as after a very challenging incarnation). God has told me I am a seraphim, and because of this I assist in the creation and repairing of souls while I'm in Heaven. I have recently been taught to do some of this while I'm on Earth. About a year ago the angels started to show me how to see and repair a soul while doing a healing on an individual. Now, this isn't something I do with each healing, only when it is necessary and I get the green light from God and Archangel Michael.

I'm told the angels that we refer to as archangels were created next and have a more varied role. They incarnate more and interact with beings throughout the universe, far more than the seraphim. There are also guardian angels, who are assigned to us from birth and are pretty much our personal angels. They never leave our sides and they assist in our day-to-day activities.

With the exception of our guardian angels, we can be contracted to work with different angels, for different roles and stages of our lives as well. When I do transitions of souls, or cross mass souls over (these are the souls of deceased humans who got stuck on the Earth plane), Archangel Azrael always assists me. He was actually the angel that taught me how to do these things. The angels I'm contracted to work with are Archangels Michael, Azrael, Haniel, Ariel, Raphael, Metatron, Gabriel, and my higher self, a seraphim I call Sere. (Hey, why complicate things?) I'm also contracted to work with Jesus and Mother Mary. I can receive messages and give messages from the other angels, but they are not part of my team in this incarnation. I actually find that clients who are meant to work with one of the angels or ascended masters who I also work with tend to be drawn to me, and those who are meant to work with other angels are drawn to people who work with them. The universe has a way of matching us with the right souls.

How many guardian angels we have depends on what we came here to accomplish and who we hang out with on the other side (Heaven). The angels tell me there is no set number of guardian angels per person. Archangels and seraphim can also act as one of your guardian angels as well. I know, I know, that's not what you have read before, but times are changing and our relationship with the angels is changing as well. There are also angels who are assigned to assist mankind when specific needs come up. I'm told that God has assigned angels to act as angels of faith right now, since faith is something that mankind is greatly lacking at the moment. When I see an angel of faith, they appear to me with two sets of wings to signify their importance in the world right now. I have been told that I'm volunteering as an angel of faith—as an incarnated angel rather than in angel form. Angels in human form have different guidelines and rules than angels in their angel form. So both are needed.

Christmas Angels

Another angelic role is that of the Christmas angel. Not only are angels here to guide and protect us, they are here to help us celebrate life and to spread cheer (think Buddy the Elf-style cheer). Ever notice how mankind seems to collectively share in joy around this time of year? Well, there's a reason you feel extra jolly, by golly! Seasons hold energy. Not only that, but we get a little extra boost of help this time of year. According to Archangel Michael and Jesus:

"There are angels working behind the scenes to grant your Christmas wishes. To bring you things like a little extra luck or good news. To bring you to someone who can help lift your burden or lighten your load. You see, the veil is also thin this time of year. All the collective thoughts of Jesus, angels, home, family and family traditions, and love carry with them an energy of love. This love energy raises the collective vibrations of those who not only share in this celebration, but to those near and far as well. It's a collective energy of joy that is not specific to religion. This temporary rise in frequency makes what we call miracles (or instant manifestation) easier to achieve and to believe. It's expected, so it is missed less often. Joy is contagious, and the angels appreciate this and offer a divine hand to all who will accept it, regardless of their religious beliefs. For love, and the divine beings who spread it, follow the love of God. And He is not bound by any one belief. He is bigger than that. He is us and we are Him."

—Jesus and Archangel Michael
Channeled by Heather Sprigg, December 2021

As you can tell, this time of year isn't special just to us. Angels enjoy this time of year as well. Although there aren't specific angels assigned to Christmas permanently, I'm told there are regular angels who enjoy taking on the temporary role of Christmas angel. These angels also work on what we call Christmas miracles. When I was working on this book, I asked Archangel Michael if I was one of the angels who volunteered to be a Christmas angel . . . he said yes. This explains why I love the feeling of magic and possibilities this time of year brings. So, how do you take advantage of this Christmas energy and magic? The angels say to "make a wish, then hold it in your heart," since that is where the angels will look for it. To do this, simply write down your Christmas wish and then hold it to your heart—and just like that, it leaves an imprint that is held there for the angels to find. If you prefer to do this a different way, that's OK too. After all, it's the intentions that matter most. Due to free will and all the wishes and prayers this time of year, I'm told the angels use helpers on Earth to get the job done. When I asked what exactly a Christmas helper is, this is what Archangel Haniel had to say:

"Christmas angel helpers are the souls on Earth you see who are doing good for others. The ones who are working behind the scenes to provide Christmas miracles and magic for their fellow humans. You see, sometimes the Christmas wish, or in many cases, the Christmas need, is something that needs to be carried out by humans. So the angels whisper in their ears and they speak through the heart of their human helper. Their whispers sound like that voice that tells you to help someone in need. The voice that guides you to lead with your heart and give selflessly. These are our helpers. And we appreciate them more than they know. For they have played a role in spreading love, hope, and healing to their fellow humans. And in return, they are filled with love, hope, and healing. This feeling, of

course, can be felt in good deeds all year long. But we are able to reach, to get through to more humans this time of year. They listen a little more, and with the veil thinner, they hear a little more. To all of you who are assisting us, we thank you."

—Archangel Haniel
Channeled by Heather Sprigg, December 11, 2021

So there you have it. I challenge you to make a Christmas wish this December, and then to keep an open heart and mind as you wait for it to happen. Please also keep in mind that there is no time limit on when our Christmas wishes can be answered. Four years ago one of my Christmas wishes was to do an event with Pat. I was disappointed when it didn't work out that Christmas. I thought, "Thanks, guys, I'm supposed to teach about Christmas wishes and mine didn't even come true?" Even though I sulked a bit, it did, however, work out the very next Christmas! It was literally a dream come true— both my mentor and I sharing messages over the holiday. The angels told me I wasn't ready the previous Christmas, and they wanted me to succeed. So please be patient and trust the angels' timing. I'm glad they waited until I was ready instead of saying "Told you so" when I flopped.

Wings and Halos

As I mentioned earlier, angels of faith typically appear with two sets of wings. This is for our benefit only. You know those cute, chubby angels we see statues of? Or the angels with big wings and halos? That's just for us. Thankfully, the image of seraphims as big globs covered in eyeballs is not correct either. (Whew!) You see, a long time ago humans needed a way to explain how angels could travel between Heaven and

Earth, so they started drawing them with wings. These are the typical depictions you'll find in religious illustrations. The angels, wanting mankind to recognize them, went along with it. Because of this, when an angel appears to us they often appear with wings. This lets us know immediately who we are dealing with and that we don't need to be afraid. As for halos, painters would often place a golden circle of light, a halo, above the heads of angels and saints in their work to signify holiness. So how do they really look? When I see them, I see them as beautiful beings of light. Usually a tall pillar of white light, but sometimes there will be color as well. Just like our souls, angels are pure divine light/energy. The first time I saw Archangel Michael with my naked eyes, and not through my mind's eye, he appeared as a tall (from floor to ceiling) beam of white light surrounded by a cobalt blue. Since I had always associated him with that color of blue, he used it to identify himself to me. Others who associate him with purple would get a purple Michael. The angels, like all of the divine, have access to our thoughts and memories. This allows them to customize how they appear to us so that we will be able to quickly identify who we are seeing. When Jesus comes to me, he shows himself looking like the image in my boys' religious studies book. At the time, that's how I would have known him to look. Angels don't have genders as we know them on Earth either. Their energy may feel more feminine or masculine, but since they are energy, there is no gender as we know it. To keep it simple and along the lines of my upbringing, I still refer to them as the gender assigned to them by mankind.

Miracles and Angel Interventions

I want to end this chapter with some examples of angel interventions and miracles. Angels are always working behind the scenes to assist us. Sometimes the angel will show up themself and appear with wings to let us know it was them. Other times they will whisper in the ear of an Earth angel and helper to get the job done. I'm told this is often done to avoid interfering with a soul's free will. Free will is what allows us to make our own decisions as we go, without interference or intervention from God or angels. These are the decisions we make that are not outlined in our soul contracts. This includes being allowed to make mistakes that are not always for our own good. Angels cannot interfere with free will, but when a soul is in human form, they have more leeway.

It's also important to note that although angels are here to assist us, we often need to ask them when we want them to step in. This isn't to say that they *can't* step in when necessary to save our lives or get us back on track (you know, slam some doors so new ones can open), but in everyday matters, we need to ask them. It's not like they are sitting on clouds playing harps with nothing to do. Nope—the angels tell me they are always working and don't have idle time (another thing I falsely believed). However, this doesn't mean they are not available to us whenever we ask. So don't hesitate to ask; after all, they were created to assist all of God's souls.

One of the ways I like to ask the angels to assist is when I'm driving, or when my family members are driving. My boys work with Haniel and my husband with Gabriel, so who I ask varies. I'll use Dylan for this example:

"Please, Archangel Haniel, ride with Dylan today and protect him from all close calls, accidents, and scares. Please take the wheel, brakes, or gas to prevent any close calls, accidents, and scares. Please also protect him from himself and others, inside of the car and out."

This really does work. On my way to pick up dinner one day, I had asked Michael to be with me just like I did for Dylan above. So as I was driving down a six-lane road, I started to approach an intersection with another six-lane road. The light was yellow, so I started to slow the car down. When I went to press my foot on the brake, however, my foot stayed on the gas. It didn't want to come off; it felt like it was being held there. At that moment I heard, "Go!" So I did. Right through the freaking red light. Once I made it through the intersection, I recognized Michael's energy signature and asked him what that was all about. He said, "You asked me to take the wheel, brakes, or gas to prevent any close calls, accidents, or scares. And I did." He told me I could have forced my foot up—I still had free will—but I would have ended up in an accident. By getting me through the light at that time, I was now in the clear.

Another example I have was when I was seven months pregnant with Cameron. This is one of those times they intervened without my asking. I was at a stop light at a busy intersection when the light turned green. I placed my foot on the gas and the car wouldn't move. Then, right as I would have been in the middle of the intersection, a semi ran through the red light. I was in a little Honda Civic. After the semi was out of the intersection my car started to move forward. I was later told Cameron and I would have died in the crash, but since it wasn't our time, they intervened. The difference in these two examples was that I would have survived the first one and it would not have had a major impact on my path, so no intervention would have taken place without my asking.

Below are a few more examples of interventions.

Cameron's Intervention:

A few years ago, Cameron was driving home from college on I-5 during a terrible downpour of rain. As he was driving, his windshield wipers quit working and he couldn't see the cars in front of him. So he asked Archangel Haniel to please help him and turn his wipers back on. He said as soon as he asked for help, she turned them back on. No question is too big or too small. If you need them, they say to please ask. As long as it's not interfering with your chosen path or free will, they will assist. As a side note, there have been times when I have had my wipers not work and have asked the angels to please turn them on and they haven't. I'm told that with Cameron it could have led to an accident (highway, blinding rain, and heavy traffic), but when I asked I could still see enough to be OK.

Joe's Intervention:

My friend Joe is a drummer in his early sixties and suffers from COPD. Recently, he had the worst episode of his life. He ended up on the side of the road in his truck hunched over his steering wheel. He doesn't remember how long he had been there, but he remembers no one was stopping to help. Until this one couple drove by, and then backed up to check on him. They called an ambulance and Joe spent five hours in the hospital trying to get his breathing under control. He was told if they hadn't stopped to check on him when they did, he wouldn't have made it. When he was telling me this story, Archangel Michael told me the angels intervened on his behalf since it wasn't his time yet. They whispered in the ears of the couple to stop.

Mom's Intervention:

As I mentioned previously, my mom worked as a sergeant at the county jail. One day she was making her rounds and delivering food. As she delivered food to one of the inmates, he grabbed the lanyard her keys were attached to. Now, this wasn't your typical inmate. He was 6'4" and played basketball for the local college. He was strong, in shape, and, unfortunately, off his medications. For some reason my mom's lanyard didn't break away as it was supposed to (to prevent the officer from being pulled toward the inmate). My mom was doing all she could to hold her ground, but keep in mind she is 5'4". Right as she was losing the battle and getting reeled in, the lanyard finally gave way. The angels told me that they are the ones who released the lanyard and that the intent of the inmate was to do her great harm. Thankfully, the angels stepped in without her having to ask.

I challenge you to look back on some of your close calls and take note of all the times the angels have stepped in for you.

Angel Message

*"Keep your heart open; it's
how the angels get in."*

When the angels wish to communicate with you,
and they often do, they will enter through your
heart chakra. The angels feel at home there; after
all, it's where your soul is. A well-balanced heart
chakra acts like a welcome beacon to the divine.

—Heather Sprigg

4
Heaven Help Us

"Thinking about the beauty of the angelic world gives a glimpse of the beauty and greatness of God."
—Serge-Thomas Bonino

Walking hand in hand with my gramma Felker, I entered a beautiful rose garden. As we walked through the rose garden, I felt a sense of total peace and love. As we passed by a green rose, my gramma stopped and pointed to it. It was important; I could tell from the look on her face. "Funny, I've never seen a green rose. I need to remember this," I thought to myself. Then I woke up.

You see, this wasn't just a dream. It was a visit to Heaven to meet with my gramma who had passed years before. When we sleep our souls can travel back home, to Heaven. Not all dreams are visits to Heaven or from loved ones, but when you remember the feelings, emotions, and details, the angels say it's usually a visit. These visits are not always conversations with direct messages; sometimes they are scripted with hidden meanings and messages, like the green rose. So when I woke up, I started googling the meaning of the green rose. What message could my gramma have for me? Now, there are many different meanings depending on where one looks. I always ask the angels to guide me to the correct meaning for a particular message. The one that they guided me to was "rebirth, beginnings, growth, and hope." It was perfect for where I was. I love that my gramma can still guide me from Heaven, which she does every chance she gets, most recently through a mediumship reading by my angel buddy, Nate. She showed him my son eating a caramel apple at a fair. At the time I couldn't place what she was referring to and told Nate so. He suggested I keep it in the back of my mind in case it comes up later. Sure enough, that very night, I opened a drawer and there was a picture of Dylan eating a caramel apple at the pumpkin patch. Our loved ones in Heaven don't miss a thing.

Heaven's Address and Soul Families

You know how when you are little you look up and picture Heaven up there in the sky, just past the clouds? I mean, how else are our loved ones supposed to watch over us? Well, that's not exactly how it works. The angels tell me that Heaven is all around us, but on a different frequency. Like a different plane of existence, or dimension. It's a bit like a radio station—where we are tuned in to only one at a time, but there are many more radio frequencies available to us. In the same way, our loved ones are actually all around us, and not looking down from Heaven—we just don't know they're right there! The best part? We can travel to these other dimensions through our dream state and during meditation. Part of our soul actually travels (known as astral projection) to these other dimensions. This is completely safe, by the way. It's not like your body is left to fend for itself and you're untethered, flying out in space alone; our soul is still connected by a divine cord of light. Imagine this cord like a piece of unbreakable thread that connects your spirit to your physical body—sort of like having a balloon string tied around your wrist so the balloon can't just take off.

You know that feeling of being startled awake? Well, the angels say when we are woken suddenly, our soul doesn't have time to gently reenter our body, so it sort of slams back into it. Again, not dangerous, but the idea is that all of us leave our bodies during sleep at times.

So what exactly are dimensions? The way it has been explained to me by the angels is they are different levels of frequency. Humans exist in what is referred to as the third dimension, or the third dimension of frequency. I'm going to try my best to explain how I work with the dimensions, and what I know them to be for me and my purposes. The angels say that what they are called doesn't really matter, that it's the intentions behind it that counts. This is why different spiritual teachers explain them differently. I was taught on a scale of one to twelve, so that is what I use and, therefore, teach. I was also taught that there are multiple layers to each dimension. For example, I refer to Heaven as the fifth dimension. Within that fifth dimension are multiple layers. Where your soul ends up depends on your individual soul growth and evolution. The more growth, the higher the level your soul has access to. Let's go back to our school example from Chapter 3. Your soul family is a group of souls that you spend time with, learn with, and grow with on the other side (Heaven). It's like each soul family is a classroom. Just like in school, classmates tend to travel together. You travel to PE together, music class together, and eat lunch together. Well, soul families like to travel together as well. So they often incarnate at the same time, or close to the same time. Because of this, you also advance to the next layer of Heaven, or class grade for this example, at the same or similar time. Those souls with more soul growth and experience under their belts are the souls in the upper grades, or higher layers of Heaven. Now, just because you are in a different grade or frequency level doesn't mean you can't interact with the upperclassmen, if you will. However, those upperclassmen must come down to visit you. You need to advance to the next level in order to visit the higher grades. This is not to divide; it's more of a frequency issue. For human souls to get the most growth, they must do it in layers. The end goal is to be closer to God. Think of God as your graduation gift (best gift ever).

When I was working on explaining all of this, I had some questions for Michael. Here is his response:

"Soul families are like kids at recess. You all come together to play on the same playground; in this case your playground is Earth. However, after recess, you all go back to your individual classrooms and grades. You will still see each other in the halls, and at other events, but you still have your individual grades and classrooms. Same school, but different locations if that metaphor makes sense. As an angel, you will return to your same grade and class after each mission, or recess, if you will, while your soul family members will advance depending on their current grades, lessons, and mission completion. This is, of course, a very simplified example based on terminology and metaphors that everyone can understand. The idea, however, is similar for all purposes.

"Yes, to answer your questions, different soul families can be thought of as neighboring schools. Sometimes students come to participate in activities at nearby schools, so there is always some interaction with other schools, or soul families. And agreements and contracts can be made between different families. The point of this message is that although levels and goals may be different, you are all still on the same campus and will still see each other."

—Archangel Michael
Channeled by Heather Sprigg, June 26, 2021,
in answer to my thoughts and questions

Diana

Diana was a close friend, and like a daughter, to Pat. Although I never met her in person, I would see her posts and feel a strong connection to her. I felt like I needed to meet her and that we would become fast friends. Even though I wasn't friends with her on social media, her stuff would still show up on my feed. It took me a while to catch on that she was part of my soul family, that my soul was recognizing hers and wanted to connect here on Earth. I'm told we are close on the other side, and did plan on meeting up on this side to work together.

Unfortunately, Diana became sick with a rare form of cancer and passed before I was able to get to Long Island to meet her. Although I didn't know her, I had permission, through Pat, to work on her, and I often did healings on her. I remember one time, I was working on her and felt so many angels step forward. The energy was so powerful that I was sure they had stepped in to give her a miracle and heal her. So I was confused and devastated a few weeks later when Pat messaged me to let me know she had passed. It wasn't until Pat told me that Diana was also an angel that it all made sense to me. Diana really was part of my family, and the reason so many angels showed up to offer support was because they were letting me know they were with their sister in her time of need.

I took her passing extremely hard for someone who had never met her on Earth. But our soul connection was so strong that I felt the loss of her energy and I felt the loss of not connecting before she went home. Luckily, I have been able to get to know her through Pat and through Diana's loving husband, Michael. Michael has opened up and told me so much about her. I'm so happy that she had him in her life and that he has allowed me into his so that I may know her through him.

Remember how I mentioned that God is sending angels of faith to assist us on Earth now? I'm told by Archangel Michael that Diana volunteered to work with those of us here on Earth as an angel of faith, to come back and continue to lead by example the same way she did while in human form. I'm also told that she is working through her husband to spread faith as well. That the bond they shared is just as strong as ever, and just like Archangel Michael guides and works with me, she will be working and guiding through her husband.

As I was writing this, Diana stepped forward and asked me to add that if you are having trouble with your faith to please call upon her and she will be there to assist you. She is reaching out and offering to work with all who need a reminder that faith isn't an elusive concept, but instead a beautiful reminder of our connection to God. My connection to her, without ever meeting her on Earth, is proof of just how strong soul family bonds are, regardless of the dimension.

Dimensions

As I mentioned earlier, how the dimensions are labeled largely depends on who is teaching you. Some teachers will label each layer as a new dimension, so as you can guess, they have a lot more dimensions in their teachings. I was taught a twelve-dimension system by one of my teachers. Therefore, when the angels work with me on dimensions, they follow that as well. Since it's all intention anyway, the system you use doesn't particularly matter. As the angels like to say, *"Different words plus the same intention equals the same results."* For example, I call where the angels are the seventh dimension, but others may call it the twelfth or five hundredth. No matter what we call it, if we set the intentions to go hang with the angels, we will end up at the same place. For this reason we can't base which dimension is really higher unless we are going by the same system. Otherwise it's apples to oranges.

That being said, here is how I use them with the angels:

First Dimension—Mother Earth

Second Dimension—Where the elementals exist

Third Dimension—Humanity

Fourth Dimension—Where Earthbounds reside as well as a portal used by other beings to travel through dimensions

Fifth Dimension—Heaven

Sixth Dimension—Where Metatron and his souls work to create new ideas and realities

Seventh Dimension—Where the angels, unicorns, and dragons dwell

Eighth Dimension—A place where we can view other lives and timelines

Ninth Dimension—The Council of Light calls this home

Tenth Dimension—Soul repair and healing of souls occur here

Eleventh Dimension—Galactic meeting space and universal counsels

Twelfth Dimension—Gateway to other universes

Please keep in mind, these are just some examples of what is done on each level. The angels want to point out that although humans use ascending numbers to identify them, a higher number does not necessarily equal better. For example, Mother Earth is the vessel of a very powerful angelic being, yet she is considered the first dimension. Elementals are also high-frequency beings, so the number two is just an identifying number (humans and their need to label and assign hierarchy again).

Higher Self

Before I go any further, I need to explain what is called your higher self. Your higher self is the part of you, your soul, that remains in Heaven. Our souls are made up of so much divine energy that there is no way all of that goodness could fit into a human body. Our higher self oversees the part of our soul that has incarnated here on Earth, or wherever we incarnate. In gaming terms, we are our higher self's avatars. (I threw that term in for my gamer boys. Mom pays attention!) This is why a medium can still communicate with a soul that has already reincarnated again. They are communicating to the soul's higher self.

Crossing Over

This is a topic I get asked about a lot. And luckily I have some experience with this. I'll give you a brief rundown, then I'll go into some examples for you. When someone passes, the soul simply leaves the physical body and is once again in their true form: energy. When a soul first leaves the body, they don't automatically get all of their memories back, or reconnect with their higher self. They are pretty much a human without a body. They still have free will, and for this reason not all choose to go into the light, or home to Heaven. However, most souls do cross into the light. They see angels and loved ones waiting on them and they head into the light with them. Some, however, choose to stay on Earth as an Earthbound soul.

Because of my role on the other side, and what I came here to do, I was allowed to go into the light. This was one of the most beautiful experiences of my life. It's hard to put into words, but since this is a book, I'm going to give it my best shot. During one of my crossing-over missions in the fourth dimension, Jesus asked me if I'd like to experience what it felt like so that I could explain it to the souls who were afraid to go into the light. After I excitedly said yes, he turned and opened a portal to Heaven. It was funnel shaped, with the opening being the larger part of the funnel. It had a beautiful golden light and energy coming from it. I felt the love pouring out of it, as if God and all my loved ones who had passed were calling me home. This feeling of love wasn't the feeling of love we experience on Earth. It was pure love, love not mixed with all the human emotions and energy we feel here. The feeling of love brought tears to my eyes as I entered the portal. As I walked hand in hand with Jesus, he told me that a loved one in Heaven (often more than one) will escort the recently departed soul into the light. At the halfway point, Jesus will be waiting to greet them. After the midway point I could see loved ones, including pets, who had passed before me lining the walls, all excited to see me. As I got more excited I began to run. When I exited the tunnel and stepped into Heaven I was hit with so much love. More than our human bodies can handle, a love so pure and all-encompassing that once there, I didn't want to leave. I was told that what I was experiencing was only a portion of what a soul who passed will feel. Please trust me when I say this: Your loved ones are not met with regret or guilt, only love. All their earthly worries and pain vanish. Once they enter that tunnel, it's the only place they want to be.

One more thing: Upon entering the halfway point, Jesus tells me they get all their memories back. They remember who they really are and all their past lives and experiences. It's a beautiful thing for a soul to experience, a homecoming like no other. Once I exited the light and opened my eyes, Davie looked over at me and asked, "What happened to your face?" When I looked in the mirror, my face was all flushed red and hot to the touch. I'm told by Jesus that it was from the intense energy of the light. It was so powerful that when my soul fully reentered my physical body, I had a physical response.

Please share this experience with any loved one who fears death. Let them know that it will be the most beautiful experience.

Exit Points

This is another topic I get asked about a lot. According to the angels, exit points are simply predetermined points in time, during our journey here on Earth, when our soul has the option to exit Earth and go back home to Heaven. I'm told the number of exit points varies by soul. When you are still back in Heaven and working with your team and planning what you want to learn and accomplish for this incarnation, your soul has the option to add exit points in case they want to come back early. The angels say each exit point has an exit window, or specific range of time that is predetermined by your soul beforehand. Again, the length varies per soul, though I'm told that kids who pass really young usually come here with only one exit point since they didn't plan on staying longer. This can be for many reasons, including inspiring change and growth in those who had the opportunity to love them.

How I understand it works is that if you have an accident or get terminally sick during one of your exit windows, and your higher self decides to take that exit, you pass. The angels have to honor your contract. However, if your higher self tells the angels they want to keep going, the angels can intervene. The only one who can override this is your higher self and God. Sometimes, I'm told, if the body is so badly damaged that the soul can't survive in it, the soul must exit and go home as well, even if they are not in an exit point. This is why it's so important to take care of your body and health. I have a friend who asked me to do a healing on her brother-in-law. I saw that his soul was burrowed into his body, that his soul did not want to exit. However, his vessel (body) was badly damaged. The angels showed me an image of an old rusty car being held together by duct tape. I was shown that if he can keep his vessel running, he could stay a few more years, which is when his final exit point is (he is in his eighties), but if the vessel fell apart his soul would have to leave early.

Another example is my father. One day, after being on the police force for about two years, he received a call about a possible prowler. His search brought him to a long, dark alley.

As he stepped into the alley, he said he was hit with what he can only describe as a "wall of fear." He said it stopped him in his tracks. He then proceeded to take another step forward, but this time he hit "an even stronger wall of fear." And at that same moment, he saw in front of him a white light shining down on a man crouched behind what looked like a dumpster in the alley. He could make out the person's outline and could see he was wearing a white shirt by the way the light reflected off it. He describes this appearing right in front of him, not in his mind's eye. Then, in his head, the knowledge that "if you proceed, this man will kill you!" came to him. He had no idea what was happening, so he went back to his patrol car to process it all. He then told himself that he was "brave, courageous, and strong," and he was going down that alley. But then the picture and warning came back to him and he thought, "How can I do this smarter?" So instead of walking down the alley, he grabbed his shotgun, stuck it out the driver's side window, and drove down the alley. When he reached the part where the wall of fear was, it was gone. He never did find the prowler; my dad believes the extra time it took for him to go back to his car gave him time to escape, or the sight of a patrol car with a shotgun sticking out of its window made him rethink killing a cop that day. He did, however, find the dumpster he was shown where the man had been hiding behind. That was some warning!

The angels later told me that my dad was in an exit window, but his soul had chosen to stay. Archangel Michael told me he was with my dad that day, and he did everything he could to keep my dad alive. But the choice whether or not to listen was my dad's. Had he proceeded down that alley on foot, Archangel Michael told me the damage from the gun would have left my dad's vessel no longer suitable for his soul. Michael says that during exit points and windows, we must listen to our intuition more than ever. Had it not been an exit point, Michael would have intervened in another way to save my dad if he'd still continued down that alley.

One more exit point story: This one is my own. In November 2023 I started not feeling well and having pain in my side. I have had kidney stones many times in the past, so I assumed that's all it was. I had no fever or chills, so I had no reason to think it was anything serious. Then one morning I went to the bathroom and it burned to urinate. I was also feeling pretty terrible at the time, but still figured it was from the kidney stone. I decided to hurry up and get my errands done so I could rest. While I was at Costco, I kept hearing Michael say, "You need to go home now." So I listened and went home. As I was putting the groceries away, I felt warm liquid running down my legs. I had lost control of my bladder.

That night I was supposed to go live on Facebook with my angel membership group, so I left a video message asking for prayers, saying I didn't know what was wrong but I just didn't feel well. One of my members, who is a nurse and is rarely on Facebook during the day to see me go live, saw that video. She called me and told me she was worried it was an infection and convinced me to go to urgent care the next day. While there, I was given antibiotics for a bladder infection and was told when the culture came back, they'd call if it was more serious or needed a different medication. Since I never heard back, I assumed I was in the clear, though I was feeling even worse and the pain was still bad.

I was scheduled to fly out to Chicago on December 13 to do an event. Even though I felt awful, I was determined to go, despite the fact that everyone was telling me to stay home, reschedule the trip, and go back to the doctor. The day before the trip, I was scheduled for what I thought was a medication check with my primary doctor to refill my regular prescriptions. When I arrived, she told me the appointment was for a regular checkup and physical, and mentioned that I wasn't due for a medication check for a few more months. She also checked the lab work from my trip to urgent care and saw my test results. Her face briefly went blank before telling me I had a bad kidney infection and needed stronger antibiotics right away. She recommended I stay home, but I picked up my prescription and boarded the plane to Chicago the next day, unaware that I was in an exit point.

Months later, as I was getting ready for bed, Michael told me I had been in an exit window then. He reminded me of the phone call from the nurse who asked me if I could come in on December 12 instead of December 27 for a med check. My doctor's office never calls to get me in earlier; that should have been a huge sign. The angels are also the ones who were responsible for the nurse "accidentally" saying med check instead of checkup. I would have canceled my appointment had I known it was for a checkup, because I hate going to the doctor and I was feeling so bad. The angels knew this, so they tricked me. Michael said they also made sure my nurse friend saw my video that day, and continued to nudge her to nudge me to get help. Luckily for me, a lot of things fell into place. He also told me had I not taken that appointment and gotten on the new medication, I would have passed away from sepsis caused by the kidney infection during my trip to Chicago.

Now, you may wonder why Michael didn't tell me I was at an exit point at the time. He said due to the rules set in Heaven, they can't tell us; they can only guide us. Again, there's that free will choice that we have!

As a final note on the topic, Archangel Michael tells me that sometimes, if a soul is determined to stay, the angels will turn their passing into a near-death experience. (NDE is when we leave our physical body and meet with our guides on the other side to determine whether or not one wants to return or end their life then.) Hey, even the angels use loopholes!

Religion

I realize this is a touchy subject for many, so please keep an open mind when reading what the angels have to say. First off, like I mentioned in the introduction, God, Jesus, and the angels were never meant to be placed into a religious category. They like to tell me they were around before religion and will be long afterward. When I asked why so many people have different views of what religion is, this is the example they gave me: God is up there in Heaven with the angels, Buddha, and other ascended masters, and everybody's up there having a big old get-together. To mark the occasion they have a photographer come in and they take a picture, a snapshot, and then God has that made into a puzzle. Then God drops that puzzle picture, and the pieces of that puzzle fall to Earth in all different places. Some find puzzle pieces that have Jesus and angels, some puzzle pieces don't show Jesus and the angels at all—you may see Buddha instead—and, in different pieces of it, you may see God; you may not see God. Although this may seem like a strange example, the point of it is that the big picture is made of all the puzzle pieces, not just the ones our ancestors stumbled upon. There is no one right way to believe; there is no one religion that gets into Heaven while the rest don't. The church I went to taught that all other religions that believed differently than us weren't getting into Heaven. That just never felt right to me.

We were also instructed that talking to angels was wrong, and that celebrating Halloween was evil and kids couldn't dress up at school. The children also weren't allowed to sing traditional kids' Christmas songs in the Christmas program, such as "Rudolph, the Red-Nosed Reindeer" or "Frosty the Snowman." They feared it would be disrespectful to God. This also didn't feel right to me, so once I realized I could communicate with angels, I asked them to explain to me why so many people believe that dogma. So they took me back to the school example and said: Picture it like a classroom with different grades. Heaven has different grades/levels; it's not just all one grade or level. Newer souls might be in kindergarten, and so they know only what information is available to them at that time. They might know only simple addition. It's all right, but there's more. And they don't know there's more until they go up to the next grade. Then they keep going up to different grades and learn more lessons and the soul continues to grow. If you try to explain there is multiplication or calculus or the things taught in higher grades, they won't believe you; they won't believe these concepts exist because they can't fathom it. Their souls are not evolved enough to fathom it. It's not that they are ignorant, but they just aren't at a level where they can understand yet. Heaven is divided on different soul levels. We graduate up to these different consciousness levels. As we do, we are capable of understanding more. By the way, God doesn't care if you celebrate Halloween or sing songs like "Rudolph" and "Frosty."

Atheists

An atheist is a soul in human form who does not believe in life after death or God. Because I know you are all a little curious about what God and His angels think of that, I figured I'd touch on the topic briefly. According to the angels:

"Atheists are created, not born. No soul comes from Heaven with the goal of not having faith. Something happens to create the need to protect themselves from what they believe will only lead to more disappointment. Some are born into families who don't believe, and they don't know any other way. Some experienced something so horrible that they lost faith in a Father who 'would let that happen.' The truth is, we are born with our faith intact. Some must lose it to find it again."

—Archangel Michael
Channeled by Heather Sprigg, February 24, 2023

The angels want to remind us that not believing in God is a fear-based reaction and that we need to show compassion for those who have lost faith, to be the light that gently guides them back.

Evolving Souls

Until recently, I believed that the amount of soul we incarnate with is the same amount we pass with. Once again, this belief was wrong. The angels recently cleared some misinformation up for me. According to Archangel Michael:

"People think of the soul as almost separate from their physical, emotional, and mental bodies. But that's not the case. You must take care of your soul's temporary place of residence, yes, but you must take care of the soul as well. After all, the soul is who you truly are. Why would you think its care matters less than its vessel? If a car crashes, don't the occupants within take a beating? Perhaps get bruised? Your body is your 'car'; your soul

is the 'you' inside. Get it now? Some incarnate with a larger
piece of them, a larger part of who they are. So yes, more soul
incarnates. Sometimes we do upgrades if a soul gets to a marked
point they set where they would need it. More 'soul' is added."

—Archangel Michael
Channeled by Heather Sprigg, August 1, 2024

Michael explains that everything runs through the soul. So let's say you came to Earth with plans on achieving a big purpose later in life, or your soul had to wait on others involved or mankind to reach a specific time or certain frequency before you could accomplish what you came to Earth to do. By the time everything lines up, you are older and it makes sense that your soul has probably been through a lot. The condition of your soul depends on your experiences and the amount of self-care you have given it. If your soul is not in the shape it needs to be in for your next steps, phase, or goals, it may be necessary to undergo a forced resting period while your soul is tended to. Your soul is your gateway to the divine; it's your connection to God and the angels. So if your soul is worn out and not functioning properly, or it gets tired (yes, I'm assured it gets tired), then it may not be up to filtering all the energy needed to come through for your next purpose or steps. If this is the case, like for my client Elisa, then you will be forced to rest. This could come in the form of an injury or illness that forces your physical body to rest so your soul can rest and heal. Elisa is always on the go and taking care of everyone but herself. The angels told me that she has more that she wants to accomplish in this incarnation and that it's time to prepare her soul for the extra energy that will be coming through. Because self-care is a foreign concept to her, they are using an injury to keep her down so her soul can be repaired. The angels say that if you continue to fight this, and do not allow your soul to rest and be repaired, then your path will need to be altered to something that your soul can handle at the moment. This is why self-care is so important. It's not a luxury; it's a requirement for soul health. So if you need permission to add some self-care into your life, this is it!

All Pets Go to Heaven

Your pets not only have souls, but they go to Heaven as well. And not just pets: all animals, no matter how big or small. I'm not sure why so many believe that animals don't have souls, but it breaks my heart that this is what is being taught. As a matter of fact, my boys were taught this in school. As you can imagine, I was not a happy mommy. I told them I have talked to many pets, including dogs, cats, horses, birds, gerbils, and insects. Another fun fact: Animals reincarnate as well. When my elderly cat, Little Boy, passed away last August, I begged him to find a way to come back to me. I told him I'd recognize him by his hair and eye color. Now, I was in a state of grief while holding my recently passed kitty in my arms and didn't think to be specific with how I was hoping he'd come back. On November 13 of that same year, Little Boy's soul was born as a blue French bulldog in South Dakota. (Thankfully he came back as a puppy and not a rat.) He was born in a litter of puppies belonging to my client and friend, Jen. Whenever Jen would show me pictures of the puppies, I was drawn to the little blue boy. I had such an emotional connection to him. I should probably add that Little Boy was a gray-blue kitty with tan and white on his belly. He also had eyes that went from hazel to green. This puppy was gray-blue with a little bit of tan and white, with hazel eyes that sometimes appear more green than hazel. Knowing what this meant to me, Jen gave me my baby back! We named him Finn, and let me tell you, Finn acts like my old cat! He likes to lay in the same spots as Little Boy, poop in the same spots (unfortunately, those are inside), and even arches his back and slaps at us like a cat. I see so much of Little Boy in him and I thank God all the time for sending him back to me. I'm told by the angels that pets often incarnate back into the same families. Usually you'll recognize a habit that will remind you of your pet who has passed. You can also ask them to come back to you like I did. Just keep an open mind and trust they will find you when the time is right.

Alzheimer's and Heaven

Alzheimer's and dementia patients can communicate with spirits, and they spend a lot of time on the other side. You know how your soul sometimes travels to the other side while you are sleeping? While there, your soul visits with loved ones and friends, and consults with your spirit guides. Your soul can also travel to the other side while you are in a deep meditation. The souls of those with Alzheimer's and dementia spend time on the other side in a similar way. They are just awake and going about their day, instead of sleeping or meditating. So when they tell you they saw a loved one who has passed, or start talking about what is on the other side, it is probably because they have been there. If they start talking like a loved one is in the room with them, it is probably because they are.

I experienced this firsthand with Davie's grandma, who was suffering from dementia. At the time I was lying in bed awake when she appeared to me, holding hands with Davie's late grandpa. She looked just like I had remembered her from years ago. I was confused at first because I thought his grandma had suddenly passed away, so I started crying and telling her that I was sorry and that "Davie wanted to come see you again" over and over. She leaned over his sleeping body and ran her hand lovingly over his head and said, "It's better this way." She may have tried to tell me more, but I was a blubbering mess and couldn't focus on anything other than her being gone. After a few more seconds, she grabbed her husband's hand again, and just like that, they vanished. As I laid there, I noticed the energy felt different from a regular visit, but I wasn't sure what that meant. I also want to mention that my husband slept through all of this. Not even my sobbing woke him up. The next morning I told Davie what I saw and suggested he call his grandma. To my relief Davie finally got ahold of her, but due to her dementia, she didn't remember or recognize anything he was saying. Despite this, he still wanted to tell her that I had seen her and Grandpa last night. Since he was afraid of confusing her, he just said, "Heather can see spirits, and she saw Grandpa the other night." And guess what? She remembered seeing both me and Grandpa, and that was the only time during the conversation that he heard coherent recognition in her voice.

To everyone who loves someone suffering from Alzheimer's or dementia, or who has lost someone who did, I hope that this story will bring you some comfort. A lot of the time, people who are close to death can also see those who have already passed as well. I think of it as a beautiful gift to those who are getting ready to go home.

Angel Message

"You must surrender your belief about an outcome to be able to recognize the miracles taking place on your behalf."

—Heather Sprigg

5

Living Your Passion-Filled Purpose

"I take joy in doing your will, my God, for your instructions are written on my heart."

—Psalm 40:8

I found myself intrigued, but slightly nervous, as I sat at a long table in the ninth dimension. I was sitting before my Council of Light. I am told by the angels we all have a council filled with those who assist us along our journey as well as assist all of mankind with their contracts. The Council of Light would be like having a meeting with all of your higher-ups. So you can see why I was nervous as I sat there wondering why I was brought here. This is the room where I'm told they take incarnated souls, angels or not, when they need to go over our soul contracts with us. This can be to make changes or to remind us of what we wanted to accomplish before incarnating. We normally do this in our sleeping hours through soul travel, or astral travel. I, however, was wide awake and in a meditative state. I was able to look around the council, but what I was able to see was limited. I knew there were angels present, a lot of them. And I know God was there as well. God and the angels were in their true forms, light. Imagine a body made of light—at least that's how I saw them.

They handed me two contracts. I had come to a place in my journey where I could choose one of two planned paths. One would allow me to live a quiet and simple life, but still achieve my purpose, and the other would allow me to play a leading role. It would allow me to lead the way for other angels to come forward while bringing people back to faith. This role is designed to help remove the belief that angels don't incarnate as humans. And, of course, to teach humanity more about the angelic realms and how things operate in those other dimensions. The choice was mine. Each contract had their pros and cons. I chose the leading role—knowing I will be judged, criticized, and called crazy. I chose it anyway. After all, each new reality comes with those who are not ready to move forward. I can only hope to plant a seed for them. For those who are ready, I hope you enjoy taking this journey with me. We are just getting started. Now for the part you are most likely waiting for: What exactly is a "purpose" and how do you find yours? According to the angels:

"Your purpose is your passion. Your passion was placed into your heart and soul as a road map to your purpose. As long as you are doing what you are passionate about, you will be aligned to your purpose. Your first purpose is the same as everyone's: to come to Earth and bring light. You do this by simply incarnating. You see, since we all have a piece of God in our soul, when we incarnate, we are bringing His divine light and love to Earth."

—Archangel Michael
Channeled by Heather Sprigg, January 16, 2024

Just by coming here you have already completed one of your purposes. See? There's no need to beat yourself up over your purpose! You are already halfway there, you overachiever, you!

According to the angels, although our passion can take us down many different paths, as long as we are doing something aligned with it, we are good to go! Contrary to what the suppressors—those who work in the dark and against the light—would like us to believe, you can't get it wrong. You may have even come here with multiple passions. This doesn't mean you are an indecisive soul on the other side; it means you were open to feeling it out and seeing where you are needed at this time. Many come here with the option to pick passions based on where mankind currently is. Mankind may not have advanced to where you thought they'd be when you picked your top passion. The angels see so many humans stress about their purpose. It was never meant to cause stress or to be some elusive goal that seems constantly out of reach. When I ask my clients what kind of target they picture when it comes to their purpose, they often picture a small target that can be easy to miss. Like you need to hit the center circle when playing a game of darts, and if you don't, you lose the whole game. That's not true at all. The target is actually quite large and hard to miss. As long as you are somewhere within that target, you are good to go! With our freedom to choose how we align with our passion comes the freedom to decide how far to take it. We all have free will, so I could have chosen to become a lawyer anyway. In that case, I would have ended up in the ninth dimension rewriting my contracts. Our soul always calls the shots. That's how we learn and grow. And soul growth is the goal. How we do it is up to us . . .

Some souls choose passions that put them in harm's way or get them harshly judged, like Dr. Martin Luther King Jr., but he was following his passion for equality and justice. He was aligned with his purpose. Souls who choose to take their passion to that kind of level bring the big energy needed to ignite the dormant passions in others. In a way, they give others permission to think big. Let's look at medium Theresa Caputo. Her passion, and therefore purpose, was to be a messenger for spirits on the other side, and to use her gifts to provide healing and closure. She could have continued to do this out of her house and in small venues and would have lived a quieter life. She would have still hit her purpose target. Instead, she took her passion and opened the doors to other mediums, including myself, to come out with their gifts. She also reaches millions of people and helps remove some of the stigma surrounding speaking to spirits. She assisted in igniting the passion in hundreds of mediums. Without her taking her passion to this level, the angels say many would have chosen to skip their top passion, or played it smaller than they had originally planned before incarnating.

No Small Roles

In fact, as I'm writing this, the angels are channeling more details to me. They are saying to picture a soul family. Within that soul family you may have a soul who wants to do something big, challenging, or downright hard this time around. So the soul family members who choose to incarnate with that soul (not all incarnate each time) may choose to play a more supporting role. Therefore, their passion and purpose is to assist and be a support to their family member. Keep in mind that soul families are not limited to your actual Earth family. Sometimes a soul family member may be a best friend who comes into your life just when you need them the most, or a neighbor who plays a role in your soul's journey. The angels also showed me that my husband came here to play a supporting role in my chosen path and the paths of others. For example, he recently had a middle-aged client who got upset when he found out his wife earned double what he did. (How he just discovered this is a mystery to me.) Davie intervened and reminded him that marriage is teamwork, not a competition. This hit home with the man and he was smiling and seeing it in a new way by the time he left. It's also worth noting that Davie is not a therapist; he is in sales. But he uses every opportunity to spread light and support his fellow humans every chance he gets. He makes a difference every day. It's important to remember that our specific jobs or careers don't mean we can't use our spiritual wisdom or insights to help others. Sometimes the things we say to coworkers, clients, or bosses are just as vital. Many times, awakened humans will find their own ways of teaching their fellow man, even if their job doesn't necessarily align with something spiritual. We all have roles to play—and even the mail carrier might have just the right words you need to hear.

Now, I know what some of you are thinking. What if I am a teacher, or a garbage collector? Or a grocery store clerk or stay-at-home parent? Am I following my passion? Am I in my purpose target? Am I here to play a supporting role? The angels say the answer lies within your underlying "why." They stress that no purpose is more honorable than another. We need to keep in mind, this isn't our first rodeo. We may have planned a more intense purpose in our last incarnation and are choosing to play a more supportive role in this one. Just like we may have sacrificed a lot in this lifetime, so in our next one, we are going to pull back and relax a bit. So please don't judge yourself or others based on purposes and passions. Remember, we are all more than this incarnation. The angels say it's also important to realize it's about give and take and taking turns. The angels want to remind us that we can't all have leading roles each time (nor do our souls actually want them). They also note that supporting roles are not necessarily easy. You still have personal soul goals and lessons to learn for your individual soul growth. There is no easy purpose, just different ones.

That being said, I know many teachers who teach because they love to nurture growing minds and working with children is a passion of theirs. They are laying the foundation for future generations. I'd say that's an important purpose. See how that works? Working with children is their passion, so being a teacher falls nicely into their purpose target. So would being a babysitter, nanny, school bus driver, pediatrician, etc. Let's do another example and take the garbage collector. Let's say his passion is Mother Earth and taking care of her. (Side note: Any job working with nature is a big deal in the eyes of God.) So working as a garbage collector falls into his intended target. He is passionate about keeping our land clean, and being a garbage collector is how he is doing it. Volunteering to pick up trash would also fall within his purpose, as would being a park ranger. Are you getting the idea? Let's do one more. Let's say you are a cashier but your passion is creating art that inspires people. The job as a cashier is how you make money to allow you to work on your passion. Your passion is inspiring others; your avenue for that is your art. Your purpose doesn't have to be linked to a paying job, or any job. It can be a hobby or volunteer work. That's your free will at work. You get to decide how to turn your passion into a purpose. The angels say working with children, nature, animals, and the elderly is a worthy calling and should be considered an honor.

The angels want to remind us that:

"No purpose is more honorable than another. They all serve an important part of the bigger picture. Raising the frequency of the collective is a team effort! Whether you live your passion-filled life quietly or publicly, you are still doing what you came here to do."

—Archangel Michael
Channeled by Heather Sprigg, January 16, 2024

You get to decide. Isn't free will a beautiful thing? The main takeaway is that if finding your purpose is causing you to lose sleep, then you are not following your passion. It's not complicated: It's what makes you feel good. When you feel good, your frequency rises and you spread more light. And that, my friends, is the reason we are here. More light means a higher collective frequency. A higher frequency means we are getting closer to the frequency of God: the frequency of love.

"Humans spend so much of their precious time trying to figure out their purpose. They ask for signs and then feel let down when they don't recognize them. Your biggest sign? Your heart's desires. Listen to your heart; it is a divine gateway to your higher self. No one knows you better. Do you want to know if you are on your right path? Ask yourself, 'Am I happy?' If you answer yes, you are on the right path."

—Archangel Haniel
Channeled by Heather Sprigg, December 2021

Angel Message

"Not every divine detour is a redirection."

Many are going through a lot right now. So sometimes the angels will provide you with a brief detour so that you can rest and heal.

—Heather Sprigg

6

A Wing and a Prayer

"A prayer is a mode of communication with God. If meditation is listening to God, then prayer is talking to God."

—Pat Longo

"**N**ow I lay me down to sleep, I pray the Lord my soul to keep. If I die before I wake I pray the Lord my soul to take. Please, God, protect everyone I love!" That was my first prayer and remained the one I used for many of my childhood years. How many of you had a similar prayer?

The very word *prayer* causes many to think of religion and recoil. However, prayer is not religion. Prayer is simply the name mankind has given to speaking to the divine. According to Archangel Michael:

"Prayer is all-encompassing and not discriminating or isolating. Prayer is the act of speaking to God, His angels, and all of the divine. Call it by another name if you must, but as long as the intention is to speak to God and His divine, you are 'praying.'"

—Archangel Michael
Channeled by Heather Sprigg, October 2023

And that, my friends, is what God and His angels want!!

It used to be that when someone offered prayers we were grateful. Praying for someone was a way to help them and show you cared. People understood that prayers could heal and lead to miracles. Now, unfortunately, prayer seems to be becoming something of the past, kind of like faith. I see it all the time: Someone will post on social media that they need help, or share an injustice in the world, and people will offer prayers, only to be told to "actually do something to make a change instead of just praying." It appears that, to many, the act of praying has lost its power. They have no idea how wrong they are. The angels tell me that when you, through prayer, ask God and His angels to send healing, love, peace, light, etc., to a specific person, situation, or place, they do it on your behalf. Each and every time. So if you pray daily and ask God to send healing and comfort to someone, He will do it each and every time. And let me tell you, it adds up! No prayer goes unanswered or unheard. I'm told that sometimes, due to the soul contracts of those involved in the prayer request, prayers have to be altered or set aside until they can be answered. But they are never ignored. I have had clients come to me, and Archangel Michael shows me a huge folder with their name and "prayers" written on it. This is the sign he uses to tell me that they have been praying and praying but are feeling their prayers are not being received. Please trust that they are.

Prayer is our most powerful tool in changing the hate and destruction on Earth. Can you imagine if everyone prayed for peace and light? For each prayer, the angels and God would act on our behalf. That would be a lot of peace and light, so much that the angels tell me we could change the frequency of Earth by prayer alone. Unfortunately, the suppressors (yep, them again) know this and are doing all they can to turn people against praying. The goal of the suppressors is to remove faith. Without faith, the desire and belief in prayer is going away. And as you can see, the consequences are dire.

Before we go any further, I want to address what some of you are probably thinking: "Why don't the angels and God send prayers on our behalf without us having to ask?" That's a good question. What I am told is that we are here on Earth to learn lessons and grow. Part of learning and growing is having free will. Everyone has free will, even the suppressors and those working on their behalf. In a sense, this is our mess; we need to take the lead in cleaning it up. Same with Mother Earth: She could very easily rid herself of the toxins being inadvertently and purposely used to poison her. But it's not her job. It's ours. And the time has come to get serious about protecting our planet. So, what can you do as an individual? You can pray for all those who are hurting. You can pray for the angels and God to send healing to Mother Earth. You can pray for peace and love and light to be sent to places that are in conflict. You can pray for comfort for those who are grieving or have lost their way. You can pray for anything you feel called to pray for. You can also pray to, or for, Mother Earth. She is a divine being with Earth as her vessel. Her energy feels very angelic to me. Every prayer counts.

Manifesting vs. Prayer

I also want to touch on manifesting versus prayer. Many confuse the two. When you manifest, you are using your intentions to cocreate your reality with the universe. My mentor, Pat Longo, said that thoughts are energy as well. So, when we manifest, we are sending energy into the universe, and the universe sends back to us what we send out. When we pray, we are requesting divine assistance. Manifesting will never take the place of prayer, as they are not meant to be the same. However, you can combine the two. Pat suggested using manifesting as a different way to pray, and reminds us to always thank God in our manifestations, as if it's already on the way. For example, here is a prayer/manifest combo that I have used when traveling to Pat's psychic fairs:

"Thank You, God, for blessing me with a safe flight to New York. I will have a fun and safe trip and help deliver angelic messages to all who need them at the psychic fair."

It's as simple as that. Furthermore, prayer doesn't have to be formal. God does not require formality. You do not need to pray a certain way. You simply need to speak from the heart. You don't even need the words. You can simply ask God to read your heart, and He will.

As I stopped working on this chapter and opened Facebook, the first ad I saw was "Prayers for peace are not enough. Please help us so that these families can see their loved ones again." This is exactly what the angels are referencing. The ad said, "Prayers are not enough." That is a manipulation. If you donated to that ad, do you know exactly where your money is going, or that it will even help someone's loved ones get home? Is your faith in people you don't know stronger than your faith in God and His angels to help get the job done? The angels and I are not saying to not donate to a worthy cause. If you feel called to donate, then by all means, do so. The angels just ask that you don't let your donation take the place of your prayers, and don't let anyone make you feel your prayers are not enough. Every prayer matters. And the angels are grateful for any and all prayers that come from your heart.

Here's another reason to pray. According to the angels, "Prayers are the gateway to miracles." Another way I like to pray is to ask God for protection. This is something I learned from Pat back when I was learning how to protect my energy. She taught me to ask God to "please surround me in a big bubble of your protective white light and healing energy." According to the angels, that is a prayer, and being the good student I am, I ran with it and now ask God to bubble everything! Did you ever play Bubble Bobble? My mom was obsessed with that video game and would make my sister and me take turns playing it with her. In the game we were dragons who blew bubbles out of our mouths and surrounded everything in bubbles. That is what I feel like: like I'm in a real-life Bubble Bobble game. I even bubble people I see walking down the street, or cars driving next to me, to protect them. I came up with a shortcut with God. I asked him to protect and bubble everyone I pictured in a bubble so I didn't have to say it each time. I just have to picture them in a bubble. I bubble my family, I will bubble an airplane if I'm flying, our cars, our pets, etc. Some may say I'm a bubbling maniac.

Prayers and Energy

Another prayer the angels want me to mention is the Lord's Prayer:

Our Father, who art in heaven,
hallowed be thy name;
thy kingdom come,
thy will be done
on earth as it is in heaven.
Give us this day our daily bread,
and forgive us our trespasses,
as we forgive those who trespass against us;
and lead us not into temptation,
but deliver us from evil.
For thine is the kingdom,
the power, and the glory,
for ever and ever. Amen.

This is one powerful prayer! Words, seasons, songs, names, and prayers all have energy attached to them, energy that has been building up through time. The Lord's Prayer is so powerful and can be used for protection. The prayer has been used since the time of Jesus and has been acquiring energy of protection and strength since it was first spoken. Every time it is used for protection, it becomes more powerful. This is why the prayer works for getting rid of negative energy and spirits. The energy attached to it is that powerful. The energy is so powerful, in fact, that saying the prayer also balances your chakras. I have tested this over and over and each time the person's chakras become balanced. Chakras are life force energy centers in our body. Pat talked a lot about this in *The Gifts Beneath Your Anxiety*. I recommend checking it out.

Michelle's Prayer:

Two years ago Michelle took her husband to the emergency room with chest pains; he was told it was pneumonia and was sent home. The next day they had to call 911 because he couldn't breathe. When he reached the hospital they took one look at him, rushed Michelle out of the room, and immediately put him under and inserted a chest tube. It turns out it had been a collapsed lung the whole time. They told Michelle that waiting even ten to fifteen minutes more would have been a different outcome. The whole time her husband was being worked on, Michelle was praying to God and continues to thank Him every day for saving her husband. When I asked her if she felt God with her when praying, she said yes. Now, I know some of you are wondering how she knew it was God answering her prayers and not just the medical team that saved him. The angels say that people who pray simply know. It's a feeling that comes over them when God answers their prayers. I can validate this as well. I can't fully explain the feeling you get, but you know when your prayers are answered as a miracle.

Angel Message

"Have faith in those whom you have entrusted your prayers with."

When you feel forgotten or like no one hears your prayers, remember that the whole picture hasn't been revealed yet. You are never forgotten or ignored. Have faith in divine timing.

—Heather Sprigg

7

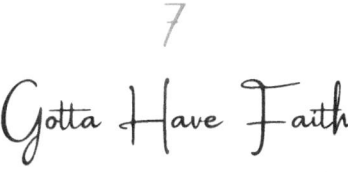

Gotta Have Faith

"We live by faith, not by sight."
—2 Corinthians 5:7

As I was sitting on the couch doing my panic breathing while trying not to have a full-blown panic attack, my youngest son, Dylan, walked up to me and showed me the bracelet on his little wrist. It said:

"I can do all things through Christ who strengthens me."

—Philippians 4:13

As I got in my car and drove toward the DMV for my driving test (new state, new test), I repeated the verse over and over in my head until it calmed me down. By the time I reached my destination, I was not only calm, but I believed I could do all things through Christ. Guess what? I aced my test. I believe that the angels nudged Dylan, who was in elementary school at the time, to show me his bracelet. I still have his little bracelet to this day. I keep it in my purse for when I need to read it.

Faith and Prayer, a Match Made in Heaven

Faith, this is a big one! You see, Archangel Michael says praying in itself involves faith: Faith that God and His angels are listening. Faith that they have your best interests at heart and will answer your prayers in the best way possible for you and your loved ones. Faith that if your prayers are not answered when you wanted them to be, or exactly how you wanted them to be, there is a reason. Faith that God and His angels love you and your loved ones so unconditionally that they would stick to your original soul contracts that you entrusted them with and would rather risk your temporary disappointment in order to help you complete what you came here to complete, so you don't have to repeat those lessons and experiences again. Faith that God loves you and knows you best. Faith is so important that God Himself provided this channeled message on it:

> *"Feeling stuck? The key to feeling free is to take a leap of faith. A leap of faith will not only launch you toward your next phase in life, but it will put the control where it needs to be. A leap of faith is saying, 'God, I trust You. I trust that You know best. I trust that after I leap, I will land exactly where I'm meant to be. Even if it's just a transitional step, I am further than I would have been had I stayed stuck and stationary. Growth does not happen when we are stuck.'"*

—God
Channeled by Heather Sprigg, July 1, 2022

Channeling messages from God always leaves me feeling teary, humble, and perfectly at home, all at the same time. His energy signature, for me, lights up all the angels' energy signatures at once and then goes straight to my heart. It's truly an honor. One that I need to pinch myself for each time and ask, "Did God really just take the time to personally talk to lil' ol' me? The dyslexic girl from Winlock, Washington?" Talk about a leap of faith!

My Leap of Faith

The first time I heard God's voice, that I actually remember, was in 2000. As it turned out, this would be my biggest leap of faith ever. When Cameron was almost two, he was diagnosed with severe infantile scoliosis. His little spine was curved to the left at 84 degrees and resembled the letter C. Infantile scoliosis, unlike juvenile or adolescent scoliosis, is fatal if not aggressively treated. I can still remember sitting in the orthopedic surgeon's office like it was yesterday. He was giving us the available options for treatment. At the time, this included fusing his spine or growth rods. As I sat there listening to the doctor tell me what my baby had to look forward to, I heard a voice within, God, tell me he would be OK, and that he would not need surgery. I told the doctor what I just heard. I must have sounded convincing because my mom and husband stood up and said, "Let's go then." The doctor laughed at me and said sarcastically, "Good luck with that."

My youngest son, Dylan, was born a couple years later with the same diagnosis. I had actually been told that there was less than a 1 percent chance that Dylan would have infantile scoliosis as well. Guess what? Being the overachiever that he is, Dylan not only had infantile scoliosis, but his curve also went to the left (not as common) and was just one vertebra off from his big brother's. Doctors were baffled. Well, not only did neither of them need surgery, but due to three Earth angels, they became some of the first kids to be cured without surgery in the US. This became one of the hardest times of my life. Treatment involved plaster casts and a whole lot of faith that I was doing the right thing. Every time I started to doubt, I'd remember the voice in the doctor's office. I could also feel the divine guidance and support of the angels who were always with me, helping when I needed them. I just didn't know it yet. In 2015 the boys' scoliosis journey finally came to an end, after roughly fourteen years of treatments. No surgery needed.

Restoring Faith

One of my purposes is to help restore faith in God. The angels say that faith is at an all-time low. This is exactly what the suppressors want. Without faith, people rely on whoever is offering help, usually a being working for the dark, but disguised as the light. Another disturbing trend that has been happening for thousands of years, according to the angels, is the belief that God wants us, His children, to come to Him out of fear. That couldn't be further from the truth. You see, God is the frequency of love. There is only love in Heaven and all the dimensions of Heaven. So why would He require fear to get to Him? The angels want to stress that fear will not get you closer to God. In fact, it only increases the divide. The suppressors have been around and working on this for a long time. And boy, can they be convincing! Think about it, though: Why would God want us to fear Him? How is that love? God loves you just the way you are, mistakes and all. The suppressors don't play by the rules; they lie and manipulate. By keeping you in fear, they can keep themselves in control.

*"There's a virus out there spreading more quickly than any
before. That virus is fear and it is deadly. Fear is the only
virus that can be spread through our computers, TVs, radios,
and newspapers. It is instantly transmitted, and once infected,
it spreads rapidly. It is often mistaken for anger, hatred,
judgment, or ego. The only cure is faith and love. It stops
the fear virus in its tracks and prevents further spreading."*

—Archangel Michael
Channeled by Heather Sprigg, February 2023

An Angel's Faith

Faith is believing in something that you cannot see. Or, in
the case of incarnation, remembering you have seen God. I'll
admit, I have an advantage in this area. I don't have faith.
You see, I remember God and being with Him as an angel
in Heaven, and not only that, I channel Him now. So I don't
need to have faith that He is there; I *know* He is. And that,
my friends, is a beautiful feeling that I pray you get to experience as well.

I want to share the story of the cabbage white butterfly (referred to as the white butterfly from here on out). The
white butterfly is known to many who garden as an invasive
pest since, while in its caterpillar stage of life, it eats greens
such as cabbage, broccoli, and cauliflower. It is said that the
white butterfly was accidentally introduced to America from
Europe around 1860 and, ever since then, has been continuing to spread and to grow in population. The angels, however,
tell a different story. They say the white butterfly is meant to
be a reminder to have faith and that the reason there are more
and more appearing is due to the fact that humans need faith

more than ever right now. They say the growing number of countries with white butterflies is no accident. Along with carrying messages of faith, they bring with them an energy of innocence, hope, and a reminder that times are changing. I like to think of the wings of the white butterfly as a pure white canvas just waiting for us to fill it with our hopes and dreams. So the next time you see a white butterfly, it could be the angels reminding you to have faith.

Not only am I a big fan of white butterflies, I am also a huge fan of Hallmark Christmas movies. So when I was watching *A Shoe Addict's Christmas* and heard the story the main character's (Noelle) guardian angel (Charlie) told her, I knew I had to add it to this book. It's a great example of not only taking a leap of faith, but how God and His angels rely on Earth angels to assist us in completing our goals and dreams.

A man was trapped in his house during a Christmas Eve blizzard, so he prayed to God to save him. As the snow kept rising, a man in a sleigh offered to give him a ride to safety. Instead of getting on the sleigh, he told the man that he had faith God would save him. After a while, the man with the sleigh came back and offered him a ride once more. Once again, the man refused and continued to wait for God to save him. The snow was now up to the man's chin, and once again, the man with the sleigh came by and offered him a ride. Insisting that God would save him, the man refused yet again. Unfortunately, the man died in the blizzard.

When he got to Heaven he asked God why He didn't answer his prayers and save him. After all, his faith never waivered. God replied, "I sent you three sleighs!"

The sleighs represent opportunities that are often presented to us, or come our way. The main reason we miss our sleighs is because of fear. Fear of taking a chance, fear of judgment, and fear of failing. These sleighs, or opportunities, are often sent by God to answer our prayers and help get us on track. Through faith, we can learn how to not only recognize our sleighs, but how to jump aboard so that we don't miss opportunities being sent our way.

> *"Believing in God and having faith in Him are two different things. Believing is the first step."*

> —Archangel Michael
> Channeled by Heather Sprigg, March 2023

> *"It is in the absence of faith that miracles seem impossible. With faith, however, miracles are a part of life. They are there when you need them and recognize them for what they are."*

> —God
> Channeled by Heather Sprigg, February 2024

When you view the world through the lens of faith, you view a world filled with miracles and God's love. How will you choose to view the world?

Angel Message

"Faith is timeless."

The angels say you are not running out of time;
you are simply running out of faith. Luckily, it's
an easy problem to fix. Start by trusting that God
and His angels have your back. With support
like theirs, there's nothing you can't do.

—Heather Sprigg

8
Judgment

"Compassion begins where judgment ends."
—Jesus
Channeled by Heather Sprigg, January 25, 2024

L et me guess, you're judging this chapter before even reading it, aren't you? All joking aside, this is an important
one that hits close to home for me. The angels will often
bring topics to light by having me experience them either
over and over or to the extreme until they soak in. This example was a big extreme smack to the noggin.

A few years ago I had an angel reading session with a
new client. This client came on like a hurricane from the
moment she jumped on my Zoom call. She started talking
about all her experiences and I found myself trying to keep
up. I started to question what I could even offer her (which
was my first mistake). Once I started to question myself, my
ego began to kick in and my intuition took a back seat. You
see, once you let ego slip in, you have allowed an opening to

lower frequencies. Lower frequencies should not be present in our energy when we are working with clients. The lower frequency that entered my energy field included feelings of not being good enough, a fear-based frequency. This limited my connection to the angels. Once I noticed I wasn't as connected as I should be, I was able to release the ego-based energy and kick my ego out the door. Luckily, I was able to do it in time to finish the session with an impactful message from the angels.

Sounds like a happy ending to the lesson, right? Nope, that would be too easy. Once the session was over, I over-analyzed it in my mind for the rest of the night and into the next day. My ego mind was working overtime, and I found myself wondering if I had lost my angelic touch or if I believed everything I had heard. The latter is a bold move coming from someone who tells people she is a dimension-hopping angel. Then it happened. This client sent me an email with a link to her blog. In her blog she wrote about some of the healers who have made a big difference in her spiritual journey. She listed me as one of them. I instantly started to tear up when I read her words. As this happened, the angels started talking to me and I knew right then that this was meant to be a topic to share in this book.

Now, I know what you are wondering: Can't the angels teach us without having us go through every lesson personally? The answer is yes, they can. However, when you are writing a book about lessons from the angels, being able to write from the heart about personal experiences allows for a deeper understanding. It is my hope that my personal experiences with these lessons will allow you to learn them without having to experience them either over and over, or as an extreme smack to the head. The first thing the angels said to me when I started to tear up was "When you judge others, you miss an opportunity to grow." I can vouch for this, too. Once I made the decision to kick my ego out of my session, I found myself in awe of all my client had to say. And while I was listening to her explain how she works on cancer, I visually saw myself using a similar technique when I go to the fourth dimension to do healings. The next night I incorporated her technique with mine and found it to be quite powerful. If I would have allowed judgment of myself and her to take over the whole session, I would have missed out on a beautiful chance to learn and grow. According to the angels, mistaking ego-based judgment for intuition is a common mistake for intuitives. They say that once we get a taste of our intuition and how powerful it can be, we get caught up in believing that all our judgments are intuition based. Wouldn't it be nice to be able to say our intuition is always right and we don't make mistakes? Well, we are still humans, after all, so mistakes are part of the soul-evolving package. The angels tell me that until we reach the upper levels of the soul-evolution level known as ascension, we are going to continue to make mistakes as we grow. If you are reading this and saying to yourself, "My intuition is always right, so I must be at the upper levels of ascension right now," I have some news for you: That's your ego.

Although some have reached these levels, the energy of Earth is still so dense that very few have reached that level in mankind's current vibrational state. Long story short: We are not Buddha. So how do the angels suggest we start to move past the ego trap? They say, "The missing key to all high-frequency emotions is love. All other emotions are ego driven. Add love and watch them dissolve into light." To break it down: Love is the frequency of God. When you add love to a lower vibration, that lower vibration cannot exist. The examples below are all ways in which people tend to experience judgment.

Addiction

This is a topic that is close to my heart. When I was in college taking courses for my criminal behavior certification, some pretty amazing things took place. This happened a couple times: I would be watching the professor lecture about a slide that was up and I'd see something about empaths. For example, the slide was about the various reasons people end up in jail or prison for drug use. Since it was for criminology, the slides focused on the mental aspect of it. When I looked up to take notes, right there at the top of the list was "They are empaths." I thought, "Wow, this class just got really interesting." After I took my notes and glanced back up, the word empaths was gone. Later, when I asked the angels about it, I was told that there are a lot of God's lightworkers in jail for drug-related charges right now, and He wants them out. So why are so many spiritually gifted souls in jail for drug use? Here's an example: Let's say you are a child who feels what others don't, or sees things others don't. When you tell your parents, they say it's all in your head, but these feelings and spirits you are seeing just won't go away. Even the doctors tell you it's in your head or, worse, medicate you for a problem you don't have. When none of that works, you start to self-medicate so that you can feel normal and function. Yet the feelings and images keep getting stronger, so you keep upping your use. The angels tell me the lucky ones get help or get caught and put in jail. The unlucky ones accidentally overdose trying to get the voices (spirits) or feelings to go away. This paints a horrible picture, doesn't it? Unfortunately, cases like this are still happening every day, and they will continue to happen until enough people know how to help a gifted child or adult. The angels want you to look at those suffering from addictions, any kind of addiction, without judgment. Judgment is not a feeling lightworkers need. They need compassion and, most of all, the tools to protect their energy so they can function when they get out.

Gina's Story

Gifted kids face judgment from all who don't understand them. As a former gifted child, I can relate. Not only was I judged, but I watched doctors diagnose my little sister with all sorts of mental illnesses. You see, Gina's gift of mediumship was beyond what many have. She could see spirits just as clearly as she could see you or me standing in front of her. One time she was working alone at a convenience store when she saw a male customer in one of the aisles. As she approached him she asked, "Can I help you find anything?" He just ignored her, so she walked closer and asked again. This time, however, he looked at her ... then vanished. This traumatized Gina and led doctors to upping her medication until she became numb to her gifts and stopped seeing spirits. But the spirits kept trying, so she'd keep needing more and more medication. I believe if she would have been born in current times, her gifts would have been recognized and encouraged. She wouldn't have been judged by peers and medical professionals and told she was mentally ill. I pray that one day, she will allow me to help her so we can start to undo the damage that was done, because it still impacts her deeply all these years later.

When your children tell you they can see, sense, or know something, please listen to them before putting them on life-altering medications ...

Heaven and Judgment

I cannot stress this one enough; there is no judgment in Heaven. Not from God, not from Jesus, not from His angels, and not from your loved ones. God loves you just the way you are, mistakes, missteps, and all. He is well aware that one of the reasons we incarnate is to have new experiences so we can learn and grow. You cannot learn and grow without mistakes or in a perfect environment. God also knows you as more than who you are in this incarnation. He knows your soul, He knows your heart and who you truly are, and who you truly are is more than this one incarnation to Earth. I'm assured by the angels that when you pass, you are met with love and compassion for whatever led you to make the decisions you did. Yes, this includes suicides. Although I'm told suicide is never part of your soul's contract, since it is cutting it short, you are still met with love and compassion. Since there is only love in Heaven, there is no room for a frequency as low as judgment. You have nothing to fear, just more to learn. There is also no judgment from your loved ones who pass before you. So many of my clients fear that their loved ones in Heaven are judging them or are mad at them. Please know that is simply not the case. The angels reassure me that all emotions such as judgment, regret, fear, guilt, anger, etc., are left on Earth. Your loved ones have moved on and released the energy attached to these emotions, and they encourage you to as well.

Angel Message

"One of the greatest gifts God gave mankind is the ability to start over as many times as you need, without judgment from Him."

Others may judge you, but the one who matters never will.

—Heather Sprigg

9

Trauma

"You may not control all the events that happen to you, but you can decide not to be reduced by them."

—Maya Angelou

This is the part of the book where I wanted to share a personal story of past-life trauma. One that carried over into this life, so that I could share an "aha" moment with you guys and tie it into a current-life issue. To show you that I can relate. However, I can't do that. Archangel Michael recently told me that this is my first time incarnating on Earth. Now, this doesn't mean I'm a young soul; angels were created first, so my soul is as old as time. But I am new to Earth, so Michael says I have no past lives or karmic debt. Which is exactly why I'm here: Since I don't have past-life trauma or karmic debt from incarnating before, my energy is pure. This is necessary for me to have the kind of constant and instant connection to God and the angels that I do. So that I can be a voice for them, so I can be a completely clear channel. I'm told by those who know me best that this explains a lot—meaning how naive and sometimes immature I can act (thanks, Pat). This also explains why, during a past-life regression with Pat, I had no Earth past lives come up to explain my fears, just trauma from this life. Or why no one has ever read me and brought up a past life. There just wasn't any to bring up. Even akashic record readings could only find instances where I was an angel, in angel form, on Earth. So I've been here observing unseen, and learning, just not in a physical body. I'm still adjusting to this, but in case God doesn't send me back for a while, I plan on getting everything I can out of this trip to Earth. So this chapter will be based on my many client readings and what I have been told by the angels.

The angels tell me our body has the capacity to carry traumas over from past lives. It also holds on to traumas from our current life. That trauma is energy that is stored within the physical body. When I do a body scan, I see the trauma as marble-sized black circles within the body. Depending on where the trauma originated is where I can see it. For example, if the trauma is from sexual abuse in this life, or a past life, I typically see the trauma marbles in the sacral area. If the trauma was severe grief from loss or a broken heart, I will often see them in the heart chakra area. These trauma marbles get carried with our energetic bodies, over and over, until they are cleared. Where there are trauma marbles, the light cannot enter because it is too dense. The angels tell me that the time is now for our traumas to be brought to the surface and released. In order to start building the foundation of our crystalline bodies, or our light bodies, we need as much available space for the light as we can get. As these trauma marbles begin to release, they start to expand. The closer they get to the surface, the more space they take up. I can look at somebody and tell how close they are to releasing the trauma, depending on the size of the trauma marble. It is most uncomfortable right below the surface, right before it releases. Unfortunately, just before people make a breakthrough and release their marble, they will shove the trauma back down, back into a tight little marble very deep within their body. Then they feel better because it's taking up less space, back where it started. They think they released it, but in reality, they aren't feeling better; they are feeling familiarity. The energy is back where it has always been. They confuse the familiar with feeling good. The goal is to complete the trauma release. In order to release the trauma, you must feel through it. For many, this will mean not doing what you normally do to numb the feelings. This numbing can be from overexercise, alcohol, drugs, eating disorders, self-harm, gossiping, or any low-vibrational distraction. It can even be shoved back down by staying in bed all day, refusing to get up and dealing with it—or even watching movies, playing games, or scrolling on your phone to avoid the feelings that need to be experienced for the release.

In September 2023, I was finally able to release a good amount of stored trauma (yes, from this life). I did not numb it with my usual tools, which were Klonopin and overeating. I was full of anxiety, exhausted, and could not leave my bed. But I felt through it, and eventually, I released it. I knew when the release was over because I woke up one morning with a sense of peace and calm that I have not known for a long time. It was significant. With that peace and calm came clarity. That clarity brought a sense of renewed purpose. I now have a clear understanding of why I'm here and what I need to do.

Releasing can also feel like a roller coaster. You make progress, then it feels like you're falling apart. This is part of the process. It's not easy, but it's worth it. The energies coming at us are meant to trigger the release of stored trauma. I am told by the angels that they are using the powerful energy of the solstices and equinoxes to help us accomplish this. They are amplifying the energy we are receiving on those dates through intention. In 2023 a large, triggered release happened on the autumnal equinox. Anyone who made progress with releasing between the autumnal equinox and the winter solstice received huge upgrades to their light bodies. The summer solstice and winter solstice are the ones where we will receive upgrades, depending on the work that we have put in during the vernal and autumnal equinoxes. These upgrades are laying the foundation and will look different for everybody, since we are all at different phases in our journeys. We will get what we are ready for—literally customized to our needs. I am told by the angels that the vernal and autumnal equinoxes will provide energy that will trigger the release of stored trauma. Keep in mind that with the release of trauma come instances of forgotten and buried memories coming back into our consciousness. Those memories need to be faced. Many of my clients have had memories come up during our solstice-guided meditations to other dimensions, in which the angels assist in shaking loose the trauma marbles that they had forgotten about from their childhood. These often include traumatic experiences with family members. These were stored in trauma marbles and blocking light from getting in. As they release through the process of remembering, they are opening their body up to more light. This is not a competition or a race, as no one gets left behind. Go at your own pace. This way, the healing will stick. If you try to force it and rush, you end up reburying instead of releasing. The clearing of the trauma will come in phases and won't happen all at once. The angels are asking you to be patient with yourself, and call upon them if you need assistance.

Do You Believe in Magic?

So why talk about magic in a trauma chapter? Keep reading to find out. Before you slam the book shut and write me off as a devil pretending to be an angel, please take a leap of faith and hear the angels out. First of all, the angels want to clear up a big misconception about magic. They did not, nor did God, say it was bad and needed to stop being used. If you think about it, it would be like God saying, after centuries of magic being used, "Oops! I made a mistake, no more magic! My bad." God doesn't make mistakes; that's a human trait. Man did, however, use God's name to cause people to fear those with the beautiful gift of being able to create almost instant manifestations. That leads me to the question: What is magic? The angels say that it's an umbrella term used to describe being able to create circumstances, cures, healings, and problem-solving using intuitively gathered ingredients, chants, and words. The energy within these is created to manifest almost instantly.

Now that doesn't sound evil, does it? So, why did magic go from being accepted to suddenly being taboo? I was lying in bed when I heard "Do You Believe in Magic" being played over and over in my head. This is a typical way for the angels to get my attention. They then told me that magic is in the beginning stages of being brought back. I was also told that other parallel timelines are ahead of ours due to us putting magic on the back burner. This was allowed to happen because man has free will, and the choice to link magic with fear and evil has set our timeline behind those that never quit using magic. Some of the ways this was done was through religion: Organized religion has villainized magic to the point where people were and still are actively persecuted. The angels say if the word *magic* causes fear, then the programming of the suppressors succeeded.

Magic is like any spiritual gift: Whether it is used for good or bad depends on the user. The angels have confirmed that not everyone stopped using magic, however. Those behind the suppression of magic, and those who work with the dark, never stopped. This is why it's time for the white light witches to even the playing field. It is time to bring magic back for those who work in the light. They have been suppressed long enough.

Once the angels decided I'd be putting a chapter on magic in my book, they started bringing me clients and students who use the gift of magic. After telling them about their gifts of magic, and even being able to see into some of their past lives in which they used their magic, many were filled with "aha" moments that provided clarity to their childhood experiences. They understood their draw to all things magic, including Halloween. Others knew they had magic in them, but were afraid to use it because they thought they would make God mad. Upon hearing that God and the angels encourage them to embrace their beautiful gift for good and to aid in the healing and growth of Earth and mankind, they were able to move past that fear and start remembering what their soul knew all along. When I would tell people about my channeled angel message concerning magic, it would act as a trigger of remembrance for those who are ready to begin exploring their forgotten gifts. This is exactly what happened when I excitedly called my mentor, Pat, to read her my channeled message. She received confirmation chills all over her body, which she pointed out was definitely the angels, because she was eating hot pepper soup at the time. She also told me she knew she had magic in her as well. Many who used magic in past lives are carrying around trauma from their last lifetime of magic use that scared or traumatized them so much that they stopped using their gift. However, the angels say it's time to heal this trauma so that they can begin to once again bring magic to this Earth.

I can't even count the number of clients who have come to me with magic in them. It's like the angels were sending them to me one right after the other so that, through me, the angels could remind them of who they were and that they were safe to use their gifts in this lifetime. Archangel Michael showed me one woman's past life from the early 1800s. She was in a rustic cabin in the forest. She had all her herbs in containers and would make tinctures infused with her energy to heal those who came to her for help. This angered the town's medical doctors, who went to the church and complained. She was told to either stop or she'd be stopped. I was shown that she still secretly continued to help people, and was later stoned to death for her actions. When this happened, trauma was created. This trauma has carried over into each lifetime, until now. Sometimes, like with this client, just knowing where the trauma came from is enough to release it.

I also see many clients as high priestesses, high priests, or wizards during the medieval times. These clients I'm shown knew how to harness the energy from the water, moon, and fire to create powerful magic. Some for good, others not so good. Could you have magic in you? It's quite possible! Are you drawn to magic? Or time periods that had magic? Are you perhaps a *Harry Potter* fan or *The Good Witch* fan? My youngest son, Dylan, has magic in him. I've been told he was in Earth retirement when asked to come back to Earth. I can feel the powerful magical energy wanting to come out. I'm told he can control fire. Of course, right now he just thinks Mom is weird. I'm starting to notice a pattern with my magic clients. They tend to be old souls with "been there done that" attitudes, which fits Dylan completely as well. If this section about magic interests you, or lights you up with excitement, then there is a very good chance you have magic in you that is ready to come out.

Angel Message

"There is no judgment in Heaven."

Heaven vibrates at the frequency of love.
There is no judgment from your loved
ones, only love and compassion for what
you are feeling and going through.

—Heather Sprigg

10
She Talks to Angels

"When you relax your mind, you let in the divine."
—Channeled by Heather Sprigg

I'm excited to write this chapter! After all, communicating with angels has changed my life! It's also one of the top reasons clients come to me: They want to know how to develop a relationship with the angels. When this happens, it's like I can hear the angels sing! This is what they want, to have a personal and working relationship with you. My father, and so many other people, grew up thinking he was bothering the angels when they talked to them or asked for help. This is not the case! I can promise you that the angels want to hear from you—after all, they were created to assist God's beings. I'm going to break this chapter down into different ways to communicate and have a relationship with them. The idea is to start with where you feel comfortable and increase your communication as you feel ready. There is no pressure; the angels will meet you where you are.

Hello from the Other Side

If you aren't used to speaking to the angels, or are just starting to explore your divine abilities, then the angels say to start by simply talking to them. I don't mean talking to them in a prayer (although that's perfectly fine, too). I mean talking to them like you would to a loved one or friend. This doesn't have to be out loud either; they can hear your thoughts, so talking in your mind works perfectly well (and is most likely how you'll hear them respond). Since one of my goals is to avoid being locked up, I tend to stick to communicating with them in my mind, unless I'm channeling for a client.

Now, here's the part that most get caught up on: what to actually say to the angels if you aren't praying or asking them for something. Archangel Michael has suggested a couple ways to get used to communicating with them. The first is to talk to them throughout the day and share stuff with them that makes you happy, such as, "Oh, look at that pretty flower, Michael! It reminds me of my grandma's flower garden." This may seem silly, but sharing your day with them isn't silly to them at all. It's building a relationship with them, and that's the idea. Another way is to set some time aside to talk to them, for example, spending a few minutes every night after you get into bed talking to them about your day, your dreams, and what you want to accomplish the next day. The point is, there is no right or wrong way to go about it. If this feels uncomfortable at first, please be patient and trust the process. I know it took my dad a while to get used to feeling like he could talk to them about "normal" things.

As a side note, do you know why we feel like talking to the angels in this way is wrong? It's because the suppressors want us to feel this way. They don't want you to have a relationship with the angels; it's easier for them to manipulate us when we are disconnected from the divine.

Signs

Another way to communicate with the angels is through signs. Just like how your loved ones in Heaven use signs such as hearts, feathers, coins, etc., to communicate with you, so can the angels. Ever heard of angel numbers? These are numbers that people see, and are drawn to, that typically have a set meaning or meanings that you can look up. For example, 444 typically means the angels are with you, or 888 means abundance is coming.

Now for the hard part: how to tell if the signs are from your loved ones or the angels, or are a coincidence. I don't believe in coincidences, so if you see a sign, you were guided to it for a reason. This gets the coincidence theory out of the way. Before I switched to mainly angel mediumship, I did spirit mediumship. I can't tell you how many times my clients would tell me they weren't getting signs from their loved ones only to have the loved one bring up a whole laundry list of signs they have been sending.

So why do people miss signs (from loved ones and angels)? The first reason is heavy emotions such as grief or anger. The angels show me that when you are so far into grief or anger it's like you are surrounded by a dense fog. So your loved one or an angel can be right there trying to get your attention and dropping signs left and right, but you just can't see them. The good news is that once that fog lifts, you will be able to see them clearly. It's also important to note that just because you can't see or feel them, they are still there. I remember a few years after Gramma Felker passed, I was having a bad day, and the last straw was dropping my bowl of cantaloupe on the kitchen floor. I sat on the floor surrounded by cantaloupe and cried. I was asking Gramma where she was and telling her I needed her. At this point I was already a medium and used to seeing hearts when I needed her (her sign). But no hearts that night. It wasn't until I was on my way to pick the boys up from school the next day that I saw a heart on the driveway. I remember asking her where she had been the night before. She replied, "I was there like I always am; you just couldn't see me or my signs."

Another reason people miss signs is that they assume it's just a coincidence (yes, we are back to coincidences). They will see their loved one's name on a license plate on the car in front of them and instead of realizing their loved one worked behind the scenes to make that car be in front of them at that time, they think it's just a coincidence or it's too easy. Same with hearing songs on the radio or having random memories pop into your mind. Those are all signs. I know what you are thinking: "I thought this was a book about angels." It is, but Gramma wanted me to share on behalf of all your loved ones in Heaven. When Gramma says to do something, I do it.

So how do you know if a sign is from an angel or a loved one? The angels say to make an angel vocabulary list. Just like a spirit vocabulary list, an angel vocabulary list is words, songs, and images that represent a particular message. The easiest way to do this is to make a list and ask the angels to honor it, and they will. If you are clairvoyant (can see images in your mind), this can be used that way as well. If you are just getting started, or aren't strong clairvoyantly, you can use the images in the 3D way with your two regular eyes. One of my next assignments from the angels is to make a sort of field journal with a universal angel vocabulary. This way, people won't have to make one themselves if they don't want to or know where to start. (I've been there with my spirit vocabulary.) By universal, they mean once you see the images and signs, they are in your mind and the angels will use them from there on out. So the same meaning applies to everyone who chooses to use them. I'm going to give some examples below to get you started. If you already use that image as a sign from a loved one, simply replace it with something else and the angels will honor it.

> **Tulip**—New beginnings, and/or a rebirth of the spirit, are in the works.
>
> **Dove**—Your loved one is with us and at peace.
>
> **White butterfly**—Remember to have faith.
>
> **Four-leaf clover**—There is no bad luck, only situations we can learn and grow from. However, your situation is about to change for the better.
>
> **Lighthouse**—You are not lost; we are guiding you to exactly where you need to be at this time.
>
> **White feathers**—We are near and hear your prayers, and hold you in ours.

Those are just a few examples that the angels have given me. You can create your own or use the ones in my upcoming book.

Mediumship

Angel mediumship is similar to spirit mediumship, except you are communicating with angels. In order to do angel mediumship, you need to raise your frequency to a higher level than when communicating with spirits. Keeping your frequency and energy high is a must for this work. If you find you need an extra boost, you can ask your high-frequency guide (we all have one) to raise your frequency to where it needs to be for the session.

It's also important to remember angels are strict on free will, so they will not reveal as much as a loved one might. They also aren't big on relationship and finance questions (this I learned after doing hundreds of angel readings). The reason is love and money are often influenced by our free will decisions and the free will of others. So it's not always accurate to say yes, you are going to end up with so-and-so. What if so-and-so decides to get together with someone else? Then you spend your time waiting for them to love you and miss out on someone else your team has sent your way. All because of a reading that was subject to change. When doing angel readings, you don't have the evidential part of mediumship, where the spirit talks about how you both used to make pancakes in the morning or go fishing on the weekends. You don't have that kind of history with an angel, so they get right to the point. Some of you who have worked with the angels in past lives, or are one, will find it easier to do angel mediumship. One isn't necessarily easier than the other; it all depends on what you came here to do and have done in past lives.

Channeling Angels

Channeling angels is the most direct way for them to communicate with you. Channeling is a form of mediumship that takes the middleman out of the equation. Instead of receiving the message from the angel and then relaying it to your client, they simply speak through you. There are different levels of channeling; I use four. The first is simply claircognizance (clear knowing). Yep, if you use claircognizance, you are channeling. Where do you think the information is coming from, anyway? When working this way, you are still very much in control, and the link is easily broken if you stop and think. As Pat said, "When you are thinking, you aren't linking." The second level is when they do a partial takeover. When this happens I start talking really fast and my hands move a lot. I have less control but don't have to worry so much about the link breaking. The third is when they fully enter my body and speak through me. I feel like I'm a fly on the wall watching it happen. I know what they are saying but can't easily interrupt. This is a very effective way to get messages across. Automatic writing is also a form of channeling.

Since a deep level-three channeling requires allowing an entity inside of you, I developed what I call energy signatures. An energy signature is kind of like a fingerprint, unique to the individual. When I first started channeling I wanted a way to make sure I knew exactly who was channeling through me. How an individual feels an energy signature will depend on your unique spiritual gifts. (See the types of "clairs" in Stranger Danger below.) Once I developed and learned the energy signatures of those I work with, which include angels, God, Jesus, and Mother Mary, I was ready to go. In order to teach energy signatures, I can give my students and clients permission to connect to me and then call an angel in. This allows me to guarantee that the angel that person is feeling is indeed that angel. In the hundreds of people I have taught energy signatures to, only one has had a physical response. That person was Pat Longo.

"I had the pleasure of having a session with Heather recently. The intention was to open me up to the archangels that have been working with me during my Spiritual journey of Healing. It was quite amazing to actually feel these angels one by one, which allowed me to recognize them as they entered my energy field. I was told that everyone reacts differently to these

energies; my experience was a physical one. With each angel that Heather called in, my arms and hands would begin to move in a different rhythm to help me to recognize the differences in energy. It was a beautiful and amazing experience!"

—Pat Longo, International Spiritual Healer, Teacher, and Author of *The Gifts Beneath Your Anxiety*

Stranger Danger

This brings me to stranger danger. Any kind of mediumship has its risks, but when channeling you need to make sure you know who you are letting into your body/vessel. This is why I make sure I recognize their energy and use energy signatures. I also allow only angels, God, Jesus, and Mother Mary to channel through me. Anyone else can use regular medium-ship to talk to me. I recommend setting similar boundaries if you are going to do deep channeling. Lastly, how you receive messages from the angels, when not doing a deep channel-ing, will depend on your unique spiritual gifts. I've listed the clair senses below (your intuitive senses which allow you to communicate with the angels or spirits; also called clairs) and how to use them to communicate with angels.

Clairsentience: This is clear feeling or sensing. I use this clair for my energy signatures. The angels can use sensory touch to get your attention by making you feel like you need to turn around, or tapping you on the shoulder. You can also use clairsentience with your angel signs, such as fluttering in the heart meaning the angels sending love to you, or tingling in your right hand to tell you you're heading in the right direction.

Clairvoyance: This is clear seeing. This can be seeing with your eyes, as clear as looking at the person next to you, or "seeing" through your mind's eye. Like if I asked you to picture a dancing purple donkey. Did you picture it? That's how it looks. Also, a good rule of thumb is if you have vivid dreams, your clairvoyance is strong. This one can be used for literal signs, like seeing a dove (normal eyes or mind's eye), for a message that your loved ones are at peace and with the angels.

Clairaudience: This is clear hearing. This can be hearing with your normal ears or your inner hearing. Try saying, "Hey, you! Have a great day!" in your head. Did you hear how that sounded? That is how your clear hearing will sound. Most of the time it's in your own voice, just like when you said, "Hey, you." If your clairaudience is really strong, you can just have the angels talk to you without signs. I have found, however, that a lot of my clients are like me and use their clairaudience in combination with their other clairs, making signs still helpful to receive.

Clairalience or clairolfaction: This is clear smelling. For example, if you ever randomly smell a favorite flower, perfume, or cigarettes that you associate with a loved one in Heaven when there is no explanation for it, you are using your gift of clear smelling. You can use this one for signs from the angels as well, such as recognizing a rose scent to mean you are on the right track.

Clairgustance: This is clear tasting. Do you ever randomly get a familiar taste in your mouth, like from a recipe your mom used to make, or a favorite soup your dad loved? This is your clear tasting. You can use this to communicate with the angels by using specific tastes as signs.

Claircognizance: This is clear knowing. It's that feeling of just knowing something. This is the clair that the angels tell me is a light form of channeling. Do you ever give someone such great advice after they tell you about their problem that you even impress yourself? Or feel like you opened your mouth and just made up a story about someone's loved one? This is often how using your claircognizance feels. You don't have time to think of what you're going to say before it happens and are usually just as surprised as the person you are speaking with. This is one of the preferred ways for the angels to communicate with us. No signs or second-guessing or sugarcoating. Just the message. I'm finding more and more clients are developing this gift as they grow spiritually. This one requires a lot of trust, but once you get it down, it's a powerful way to receive and give messages.

When you are doing angel mediumship, you can use any combination of the above clairs to relay messages to your clients, or yourself, just like with spirit mediumship. I also believe we all have the ability to use any of them. But just like muscles, the ones we use the most tend to be the strongest. So please set aside some time and communicate with the angels. They are waiting to hear from you.

Angel Message

*"God seeks to unify, not divide.
If the message aims to divide or
cause fear, it's not from Him."*

The angels want to remind you to be careful whose
energy you work in, and whose words you listen to.

—Heather Sprigg

11

Last but Not Least

The Road Not Taken

Two roads diverged in a yellow wood,
And sorry I could not travel both
And be one traveler, long I stood
And looked down one as far as I could
To where it bent in the undergrowth;

Then took the other, as just as fair,
And having perhaps the better claim,
Because it was grassy and wanted wear;
Though as for that the passing there
Had worn them really about the same,

And both that morning equally lay
In leaves no step had trodden black.
Oh, I kept the first for another day!
Yet knowing how way leads on to way,
I doubted if I should ever come back.

I shall be telling this with a sigh
Somewhere ages and ages hence:
Two roads diverged in a wood, and I—
I took the one less traveled by,
And that has made all the difference.
—Robert Frost

've learned so much by working with the angels. By accepting my gifts and my purpose to be a voice for the angels, I found my voice. This book is just the tip of the iceberg with what I wish to share with the world. Each channeling I do for myself and for my clients brings so many lessons and divine words of wisdom from the angels, the subtle and the not so subtle. The topics covered in this book were the ones the angels felt needed to be heard the most at this time. To help you move forward toward your passion-filled purpose with the confidence that comes from looking within and finding "you." To give you the confidence to not only move forward with your dreams, but to aim high and not worry about judgment from others. Confidence that comes from a renewed sense of faith and knowing that your prayers are heard and God loves you unconditionally. And lastly, the confidence in knowing that by reading this book you have let the angels know you want a relationship with them.

I want to leave you with a few lessons I have learned along the way. These are themes that I have noticed come up in many of my angel readings for clients. These lessons have helped me along my journey. I hope that they will help you too.

#1 There are always angels around you. I get asked all the time, "Are there any angels around me that want to work with me?" I have never had the angels say, "Nope, this guy is flying solo." Until you are ready to work with them and recognize their signs, they are often your silent protectors and cheerleaders working behind the scenes to guide you. I can't tell you how many times I have heard the angels' excitement at a client finally being ready for a more personal relationship with them. Archangel Michael has been telling me that the angels have been eagerly waiting for mankind to reach this point in time again so that they can work side by side with us instead of behind the scenes. In the time of Atlantis and Lemuria, they worked closely with us, and since the collective frequency had risen to a point that the veil was thin enough for humans to see the angels with their naked eye, they walked among them. This is what the angels say we are laying the foundation for right now. This is why your work here at this moment is so important. This is why you being here and shining brightly is so vital. No light or purpose is too small; you shine more than you know and are assisting more than you know.

#2 Tough love is still love. This one has been showing up more and more as people begin to set boundaries and step into self-love. The angels say that when you are constantly fixing the problems and making all the decisions for someone, they don't have the opportunity to learn and grow on their own. Listen, as a mom I feel this one. My first reaction is to step in and try to fix everything for my boys. But they don't learn that way, and eventually they will need those skills. Whether it's your child, spouse, extended family, or friends, by allowing them to do things on their own and face the consequences of their own actions, we are allowing them to learn from these situations, and in the process, experience soul growth. One example is when an adult child keeps getting in trouble for using drugs, so the parent gives them money to keep them afloat. By the time the parent comes to me, they are usually at their wits' end. This is typically when the angels remind them that tough love is still love. When you look at it through the lens of soul growth, it makes it a bit easier to allow them to learn from their mistakes. After all, soul growth is a big part of the reason we are here.

#3 Not only is it OK to set boundaries, it's a good idea. The angels say now more than ever, setting boundaries to protect your energy is needed. Since the frequency of Earth and mankind is rising, we are becoming more and more sensitive to the energies around us. Even those who thought they weren't an empath are finding out that they are. The angels tell me that no one who is currently incarnated is not an empath. This hasn't always been the case, but with mankind being in these important foundational times, it was necessary. As empaths, we feel the energy of others even when we are not physically near them. This energy impacts our physical, emotional, and mental health. This is why we not only need to protect our energy by using the bubble, grounding, shield, and energy release techniques (instructions at the end of this chapter), we need to protect it by keeping those who drain us at a safe distance. For example, telling a downer friend who only likes to gossip and makes you feel bad about yourself that you no longer can hang out with them is setting healthy boundaries. Or telling a family member who always puts you down and makes you feel bad that you won't be at Sunday dinner is healthy boundary-setting. Now, the angels aren't saying to be mean about it, but they are saying to protect your energy so that you can keep your frequency high. If someone is constantly bringing it down, a boundary needs to be set.

#4 You are right on time. So many clients feel that they are running out of time, or that they waited too long to start working on their purpose. I'm going to answer this one with an example from the angels. Think of a classroom full of students taking their written final with a one-hour time limit. Some will finish and turn it in after just twenty minutes, and some at thirty minutes, and some at forty-five. There will also be students who will turn it in at the last second. When the teacher goes to grade the tests, they won't grade on when the final was turned in or how long it took the student to finish it. They will even give points to students who don't finish in time. This is a simplified example of how it works for humans. It doesn't matter when you start to fully step into your gifts or purpose or how much of an impact you have. It just matters that you start and try. And remember Chapter 5, about your soul's purpose? Just by coming here, you are halfway done with your chosen assignment.

The angels also want me to mention that some of us came here with the intention to awaken and remember when the collective frequency hits a certain frequency or milestone/event. You aren't responsible if mankind doesn't hit that frequency or milestone until you are eighty or even at all in your lifetime. That's not on you. So relax and just do your best; that's all God and His angels expect.

#5 Forgiveness is the gateway to peace. The angels say that when you forgive someone, including yourself, you release the knot of anger that is tying you to that person or feeling. When we are angry at someone, we often subconsciously attach energetic cords to them. This means that we are continuing to feel their energy. This feels like a big old unfair reminder of why we are hurt and angry in the first place. By forgiving them, we get rid of the cords (and stop attaching new ones) that bind us to them. The angels say to remember, forgiveness is for you, not them. They are also saying they don't expect you to forget just because you forgive. Kind of like that song "Little Rock" by Collin Raye where he says that Jesus forgives but fathers don't forget. Forgiveness also doesn't mean you have to have a relationship with that person again either. You can forgive, set your boundaries, and continue on without that knot of anger keeping you tethered to them and lowering your frequency.

I have a personal story for this one. When my boys were little I was the volunteer coordinator at their small private school. During that time I made a few close friendships with other parents and the staff. I also did a lot of secretarial work for free since I was there anyway. When it came time to switch my boys to a larger Catholic school, I was treated like a traitor and many friendships ended. I realized that it was only my free work that was keeping the friendships alive. It hurt pretty badly, especially one particular friendship. Every time their name would come up (we still had acquaintances in common), the hurt and anger would rip the wound right open again. I was trying to forgive but was having trouble, so I used a pink light technique that Pat taught me, and it worked. One day their name was mentioned and I felt nothing. I remembered what happened, but there was no longer any emotion attached to the memory. I was free. Pat's pink light exercise is below:

"Send pink light and love to people you are having difficulties with. It is always best to send a positive thought than a negative one, as it comes back to you tenfold. 'I, (your name), send a beam of pink light and love from my heart to the heart of (their name).' This will help to diffuse or resolve the situation."

—Pat Longo

#6 Your mistakes don't define you. The angels want to encourage you to give yourself permission to let go of the past and the mistakes that hold you prisoner to it. They want you to think of mistakes as lessons learned instead of mistakes. When you change your wording and thoughts from the negative *mistake* and switch to *lessons learned*, you release yourself from the negativity attached to the situation. Words, whether spoken or thought, carry energy. Something as simple as replacing *mistakes* with *lessons learned* can allow you to move forward and raise your frequency. We are here to learn and grow, so learning lessons (sometimes the hard way) is all part of this human experience and journey. And in case you are wondering, no one in Heaven is keeping track of your perceived "mistakes." That's a human-only trait.

#7 There is no need to feel guilt. In fact, according to the angels, guilt is a man-made emotion humans use to torture themselves (sounds about right). Guilt is another negative emotion that holds us back from living our best lives and lowers our frequency. The angels are giving you permission to release the guilt and move on. This is a topic I know well. The summer Cameron graduated from high school, I was suffering badly from mom guilt. All I could think about was all the stuff I didn't get to do with him. Then my mom guilt snowballed and I started feeling guilty for the times I was too anxious or depressed to take him (or his little brother) to the park, or host play dates like other moms did. I felt like he missed out because of me. After a couple weeks of sinking deeper and deeper into mom-guilt depression, the angels stepped in. They usually let me figure things out myself, but they must have figured I was drowning, so they threw me a life preserver.

They said, "Be the best mom you can be for the situation you are in." They then went on to explain to me that it doesn't matter if you are a working mom, a stay-at-home mom, are poor, suffer from depression, anxiety, or anything else. Just be the best mom (or dad) that you can be for your current situation, and adjust as your situation changes. They reminded me that no one on the other side expects any of us to be perfect. I often think of these words when I start to feel guilt creeping in. I hope they will help you with whatever kind of guilt you are carrying around. Let it go; it doesn't serve us in any way.

#8 Not every detour is a redirection. We usually think of detours, or doors closing on us, as a sign that we need to be rerouted. The angels say that not every divine detour is for a redirection. Since so many are going through so much right now, the angels will sometimes give you a brief detour so that you can rest and heal. They want you to take advantage of this divinely appointed break and allow yourself to rest . . . guilt-free. An example of this is when a client will quit or lose a job and has some trouble finding a new one. They will often tell me they have no idea why it is taking longer than they expected. The angels will often say they are giving you time to rest. Now, if you are tight on money and can't survive without an income, they will find other ways for you to rest. I have also seen them use a non-life-threatening injury to force rest and healing. The takeaway is if you find yourself with some unexpected downtime, try to look at it as a gift. Remember, the angels know what is best for us, even when we don't.

#9 Love heals. This one is huge! So many feel helpless when a loved one is hurting and they want to know what they can do to help. The angels have this to say:

"Love is the language the heart speaks. The purest form of communication between humans. The high vibrational frequency of love has the ability to heal just from feeling and thoughts. When you truly send love, you are sending healing. For love is a higher frequency than any ailment that anyone could possibly go through. There is no higher frequency than love. So in short: Love heals."

—Archangel Michael
Channeled by Heather Sprigg, November 13, 2021

When you send your love, it comes from the heart chakra, where our soul is. And in our soul is a piece of God. Don't let anyone tell you sending love isn't powerful. By sending love, you are helping them heal, not only physically but mentally and emotionally as well.

#10 You cannot disappoint God or His angels. I have a lot of clients who feel they have let God or the angels down because they haven't opened up to their divine gifts yet, or aren't using them the way they believe God intended. Please know God loves you too much to be disappointed in you. You are the ones who set your intentions and goals when you come to Earth. God is not disappointed in your progress ever. It is the suppressors who want you to believe this, because it leads to guilt. And guilt is a low-frequency emotion that keeps your vibration low and keeps you from doing what you came here to do. If you fear letting God down, or disappointing Him, you stop taking chances so you don't risk disappointing Him more. This guilt stifles your spiritual growth and puts up mental roadblocks that prevent you from fully experiencing all you came here to experience. He loves you whether or not you complete your lessons. He knows you are learning and that Earth is a tough school. Also, like we talked about in previous chapters, God knows you as more than this one incarnation. So please release that fear and allow yourself to move forward without that guilt weighing you down.

#11 Imaginary friends are real. Not only are they real, but I've had the honor of connecting a few to their childhood friends. The first "imaginary" friend I met was not long after I began communicating with spirits. I was sitting with my friend's fourteen-year-old niece, who I'll call Amy. We were talking about spirits and school when she shyly asked me if imaginary friends could sometimes be real. As soon as I said, "Yes, sometimes," her face lit up and she told me she had always felt her imaginary friend had once been alive. This kid was excited; she was smiling ear to ear and bouncing in her seat! Amy told me her imaginary friend first showed up when she was around five years old, and that her name was Gloria. She then proceeded to tell me Gloria's story. Gloria's parents had been alcoholics and had been drinking and driving one night with her and her brother in the car. They got into an accident and her brother and parents were killed. Gloria then went to live with her aunt, also an alcoholic. In a sad twist of fate, the aunt was also drinking and driving one night ... and sadly, Gloria was killed. She was fourteen at the time. At this point I was thinking either Amy's imaginary friend was a spirit or this little girl had one dark imagination. Not the kind of backstory I would expect a young child to come up with.

After shocking me with Gloria's past, Amy began to describe Gloria. She told me Gloria had beautiful red hair and cute freckles. As she was describing her, guess who showed up? Gloria! I was not expecting that; I think I was just as excited as Amy! I stopped Amy and asked her if Gloria had green eyes, if her red hair was more reddish brown as opposed to bright red, and if it was long and wavy and parted to the side. Amy's eyes lit up as she asked, "How did you know?"

I told her, "Gloria is here right now and she's definitely not imaginary." Unfortunately, Gloria wasn't interested in talking to me; she just wanted Amy to know she was real and that she was still there. She did, however, tell me she was sticking around to protect Amy, and then she left. Since I know you'll ask, I didn't need to try to cross Gloria over. Gloria had already crossed but was coming back to visit Amy.

#12 God does not punish you by making you do something over and over until you get it right. He gives you another chance. You know how when you are a child and you are learning something new and can't wait to show your parents? You go and gather Mom, Dad, and any siblings hanging around and set off to show them how you can ride to the end of the block for the first time without your training wheels. Only, instead of it turning out how you imagined it would go, you stumble and get frustrated. Now, your parents don't say, "Oh well, time to find a new hobby." Nope, they will give you as many chances as you need to get it right. And they will be cheering you on, lovingly, the whole time. Same with God. When we don't get a lesson right, one that God knows we wanted to accomplish when we headed to Earth, He simply gives us another chance to show Him we can do it. He lovingly encourages us and cheers us on until we get it right, just like any good parent would. So please remember, you are not being punished; you are being given another chance to get it right. Another chance to accomplish the goals you set for yourself in your soul contracts before coming to Earth.

Thank you for being a part of this journey with me! I hope the angel messages I have shared, along with my personal stories, will help you build and strengthen your connection to the angels while providing you with faith and hope.

Please remember, the road you walk may be long, but you don't walk it alone. There are angels beside you every step of the way.

"Your dreams are waiting. If you are looking for a sign that it's time to start making your dreams a reality, this is it! We are standing by and ready to help; all you need to do is ask."

—Archangel Michael
Channeled by Heather Sprigg, January 18, 2023

Energetic Exercises

I've listed the energetic exercises I use below. I recommend doing the bubble, shield, and grounding exercises morning, midday, and before bed. I use the quickie grounding when I'm driving or short on time. The energy release should be done morning and night, and as needed throughout the day.

Pat Longo's Exercises

Bubble

Imagine a big beam of God's white healing love and light coming down and surrounding you in a big bubble. If you would rather say it, you can do that too: "Please, God, surround me in a magnificent bubble filled with your protective love, light, and energy."

Grounding

Imagine two cords coming out of the soles of your feet and one from your tailbone. The cords are going straight into Mother Earth where they spread out like the roots of a tree to connect you to Mother Earth and ground you. You can also say, "I have two cords coming out of the soles of my feet, and one from my tailbone. They are shooting straight into the earth where they attach and spread out like the roots of a tree to connect me to the earth and ground me."

Shield

Imagine a shiny metal vest of armor that covers your heart, your lungs, your solar plexus (which is below your sternum), and down through your waist. It should cover your front and back, shoulders through waist. You can also say it: "I am putting on my shiny metal vest of armor that covers my heart, lungs, solar plexus, and through my waist. My vest protects me from all toxic or negative energy and emotions that are not mine."

Heather Sprigg's Exercises

Energy Release

Simply say, "I release all energy from my energy field that is not of me and send it back to the original senders with love. I call back all of my energy with love." I then seal my energy field with a bubble of protective white light.

I prefer to picture it, but simply saying it works as well. It's important to send and call back with love. You never want to send anything negative out into the universe.

The energy of others (living or nonliving) and places can get stuck in our energy fields. Once this happens it slowly works its way to our physical body. In order to prevent this, we can send the energy back to the senders. Ever have an argument with someone you don't really know, and then haven't been able to get them out of your mind? This is likely because their energy is in your energy field. Release their energy and see what happens!

Quickie Grounding

Ask your guardian angels and spirit guides to ground and/or anchor you to the best possible dimension and/or vibration for you.

Not sure if you are grounded? If you find yourself tripping over your words or your feet, running into walls, losing your train of thought, or feeling disconnected, you probably need to ground. My son Cameron was giving a presentation in college when he noticed he was fumbling over his words. So he closed his eyes and said the quickie grounding in his head as he took a deep breath. He then opened his eyes and when he started talking again, his words came out perfectly.

For more information on energy, check out Pat Longo's book, *The Gifts Beneath Your Anxiety: Simple Spiritual Tools to Find Peace, Awaken the Power Within, and Heal Your Life*.

Acknowledgments

Although this book was a labor of love, I wouldn't have been able to do it alone. I am forever grateful for everyone who played a part in helping this book come together.

To my husband, Davie, thank you for believing in me from the start and encouraging me to follow my dreams, even when it meant you had to work longer hours. Your loving support and sacrifices have allowed me to spread my wings and fly! Thank you for not laughing when I told you I can talk to spirits and later when I told you I think I am an angel. Lastly, thank you for being an amazing dad to our boys. I love you!

To my boys, Cameron and Dylan. Thank you both for choosing me, a first-time incarnated angel, to be your mom! Thank you both for always being supportive and loving me and being my reasons for everything. My favorite role in this life will always be being your mom. Without you guys helping Dad hold down the fort and babysit our two crazy dogs, I wouldn't have been able to sneak away to hotels for uninterrupted channeling time. Please keep dreaming big and know you can do and be anything you want! I am so proud of you guys! I love you both, more than words!

To my puppy, Finn. Mommy loves you so very much! Thank you for all the puppy love and kisses when I needed them.

To my parents, Mike and Ona. Thank you for filling my childhood with magic and showing me anything is possible. I still look for dragons when I see fog (a.k.a. dragon's breath) on the hills and mountains, and I still search the sky for Santa and his reindeer every Christmas Eve. I believe in a parallel universe Santa exists and I plan on traveling there one day and telling you guys all about it! Thank you both for continuing to support me and for being the best parents and grandparents ever! I love you guys!

To my sister, Gina. Thank you for choosing me as your earthly sister (yes, you had a choice)! I know I wasn't always easy to share a room with, but I have always loved you dearly. Your strength and determination to overcome all that this life has thrown at you has been so inspiring. Thank you for loving my boys like they were your own, and for giving me a nephew and niece to love. Tyler and Samantha, keep dreaming big and remember Aunt Headie loves you guys!

To Nathaniel (Nate) Scripture. When we met in channeling class six years ago, we knew we would be best friends forever. You are the big brother I always wanted. Thank you for incarnating at the same time as me and for all your help with this book. You spent hours going over each word and chapter with a producer's eye and added valuable insight and suggestions. I truly believe my book is better because of your dedication to helping me. Thank you also for making my vision for my book cover come to life. You are family to me and I love you.

Thank you to Pat Longo. Thank you for always having my back and being there to answer all my questions and help me fill in the blanks for this book. Thanks for reading it and making sure I didn't say anything embarrassing. (We both knew it was a possibility.) You were the only mentor and teacher, besides the angels, that I needed, and now I will fly solo with the knowledge you have left me with. Thank you for never giving up on me and for loving me. I will miss you forever. I love you.

Thank you to my friends (you guys know who you are)! Without you guys I wouldn't be me. Thank you all for the support and encouragement and for never giving up on me when I needed space to work and find myself. Thank you for being there for the good and the bad, and thanks for believing in me. From friends to sisters, I love you guys!

Thank you to Jennifer with Pen & Publish for taking me on as a client. Thank you for patiently answering all my questions and guiding me through this process.

Last but not least, thank you to God, His angels, and the rest of my spirit team in Heaven. Thank you for trusting me with this mission and choosing to channel through me. Thank You, God, for allowing me to be here and for surrounding me with amazing souls to walk this journey with. Thank you to the angels for always being with me, protecting me, and guiding me. Thank you, Archangel Michael, for being my Heavenly partner in writing this book.

On August 31, 2025, my sweet baby boy, Buggie (pug mix), passed away. He was just a couple months short of his sixteenth birthday. Buggie has been with me and comforted me through my awakening and all my anxiety. He was a constant companion in my life, one that can never be replaced. I believe the angels sent him to me to help me on this journey. My own little angel to help me remember who I am.

Buggie,

Thank you for always being there for me and loving me unconditionally. The first thing I will do when I get back to Heaven will be to run across that rainbow bridge and hold you again. I will miss your snores and snorts and how you kicked me out of the way when I took up too much of the bed. I will miss the way you were always so happy to see me whenever I got home or even just entered a new room. I am so glad you can breathe and walk easily again.

Please tell Pat hi for me and send me signs! I promise to take care of your brothers and favorite teddy bear.

Mommy loves you!

Love,

Mommy

About the Author

Heather Sprigg is an angel channel, medium, healer, and teacher with followers and clients from around the world. Her work is specifically focused on showing others how to build a direct and personal relationship with the angels. She has dedicated her career to being a voice for them, and has been divinely directed to teach about their roles with humanity. Heather developed a special system on how to identify individual angels based on their unique "energy signatures." In addition to hosting angel workshops, Heather offers angel retreats, as well as an online membership where people can open up their own gifts and also learn to develop deep relationships with the angels.

If you would like to learn more about the angels or find out about Heather's next book and her upcoming podcasts/video casts and projects, you can subscribe to her newsletter through her website or follow her on social media.

Website: heathersprigg.com
Email: heathersprigg111@gmail.com
Facebook: facebook.com/angelhealerheathersprigg
Instagram: @heathersprigg111

www.ingramcontent.com/pod-product-compliance
Lightning Source LLC
Chambersburg PA
CBHW021204130626
46554CB00005B/1971